THE ANGER FACTOR

Letting Go of Your Unresolved Anger

JEFFERY COMBS

D1562934

GOLDEN MASTERMIND SEMINARS INC.

Published by Golden Mastermind Seminars Inc.
www.goldenmastermind.com

Cover design: FlowMotion, Inc.

ISBN 978-1-934919-15-6

Printed in the United States of America

5 4 3 2 1

*Dedicated to the many individuals I've had the
privilege of coaching over the last twenty-five years*

TABLE OF CONTENTS

FOREWORD 7
INTRODUCTION 9

PART ONE: ANGER—THE BACKSTORY
One: Anger Affects Everything 18
Two: The Roots of Anger 27
Three: Why Anger Is Hard to Shake 44

PART TWO: THE EFFECTS OF ANGER
Four: From Anger to Addiction 55
Five: The Angry Giver 67
Six: Passive-Aggressive Anger 80
Seven: How Anger Sabotages You 91
Eight: Anger and Your Health 103

PART THREE: RELEASING ANGER
Nine: Letting Go 122
Ten: Releasing Addictions 147
Eleven: Forgiveness: The Language of the Heart 159
Twelve: From Angry Reactor to Peaceful Responder 172

NOTES 194

FOREWORD

In his newest book release, *The Anger Factor*, Jeffery dives deep into the heart of an issue that is rarely discussed or resolved by most people.

Anger can show up in many forms. It can be our biggest nemesis or our biggest ally when we learn to recognize it and learn how to release it and channel that energy toward the goals and dreams we want to achieve.

What you will find as you read this book is that anger can be very subtle and often can be very devastating.

In either case, getting a grasp and fully understanding any anger issues that you or someone you love has can mean the difference between living in a prison or living in the gardens of heaven.

In reading this book, I noticed that I may have some anger issues around my childhood, and this shows up as negative stories I tell myself about my past. What a great wake-up call to stare this emotion straight in the face and have the tools found in this book to accept it and deal with them.

If you really want to skyrocket your life and results, learn to release any of your known or hidden anger issues and free yourself from the emotional bondage that it holds on you.

I highly urge you to read and apply what you learn in this book, and if you have children, make sure you share what you learn with them. You'll save them years of self-sabotaging thoughts, feelings, and destructive behaviors.

—John Assaraf

INTRODUCTION

I wrote this book for all those who suffer from unresolved anger. For more than twenty-five years, I have been privileged to coach many quality, talented individuals— people with unlimited potential—who have not been able to achieve the success they desire due to the effects of unresolved anger. Instead of living lives of peace and prosperity, too often they struggle to merely get by, laboring under heavy burdens that stem from past events.

These individuals may have all the right intentions and do all the right things: they attend seminars, read books, seek out mentors and coaches, and yet they still find themselves unable to break free of struggle, guilt, shame, and overwhelm. Why? Often unresolved anger is the underlying cause that creates such effects. This is a very misunderstood topic, with very few books written on this subject.

Letting go of unresolved anger is absolutely essential if your goal is to be a balanced, successful human being. No matter what goals you set in life or what lifestyle choices you make, you share a common desire with most people to be happy, fulfilled, and engaged in life. Like many personality types, anger has its own set of characteristics, and those characteristics manifest themselves in unique ways in every individual. This book is dedicated to those who desire and deserve to release unresolved anger from past events so they can live lives of excellence and wholeness in the present.

Think about what happens when you go through a meltdown, or experience a series of stressful events, or find yourself disappointed. You might ask yourself, "Why do I do this to myself?" or "Why is this happening to me?"

The answer is *sabotage*, which is a French word originally used for a group of people called the sabots. These individuals deliberately did sub-par work as a way to force their employers to concede to their demands. Since World War I *sabotage* has been commonly used to mean "actions taken by enemy agents against a nation's war effort."[1] When you sabotage yourself, you become your own worst enemy. You end up working against your own best efforts and intentions. As Marianne Williamson says:

> *The ego mind both professes its desire for love and does everything possible to repel it, or if it gets here anyway, to sabotage it. That is why dealing with issues like control, anger, and neediness is the most important work in preparing ourselves for love.*[2]

People with emotional addictions commonly end up sabotaging themselves. Self-sabotaging behavior results from a misguided attempt to rescue ourselves from our own negative feelings. Good intentions do not always equal good habits. If you have tendencies that lead to anger based on unresolved issues from the past, there's a high probability you will set yourself up to be disappointed. Emotions that affect us neurologically—disappointment, anger, hate, resentment, guilt, shame, abandonment, rejection, and overwhelm—keep us doing the same things over and over, and we're left wondering why we don't succeed. If we don't face into these deeper issues—if we don't move beyond the effects to understand the true cause of them—we stay stuck in anger's grip.

I'm not a psychiatrist or a psychologist, so what qualifies me to write a book on anger? In addition to the fact that I have coached thousands of individuals over the last twenty-five years, I'm recovering from my own issues with anger from past events. What I share in these pages has emerged from my journey to resolve the anger issues in my own life.

For instance, I used to get so excited and so wound up and so intense that I would end up alienating people with my energy. Energy and excitement are usually seen as positive, but the particular form of excitability I exhibited was based on unresolved issues from my past. I was so intense that when I would talk, I literally would be sputtering with intensity.

My game really began to change back in the mid-1990s when I was introduced to Frederic Lehrman, a brilliant speaker, author, and teacher. In his audio series, *Prosperity Consciousness*, he asks what might seem like an odd question: "Are you willing to be wealthy?" He explains that deeply ingrained subconscious beliefs can hold us back from what we consciously desire. When our thoughts are in conflict, failure tends to win out over success.

I learned a great deal from that series, and in 1996 I had the distinct privilege of meeting Frederic at an event in an offshore location in the Bahamas. I had the opportunity to walk the beach with him, and through our conversations I gained a better understanding of cause and effect and why I did what I did. I learned how better to resolve the discrepancies between my conscious and subconscious mind.

I was an alcoholic for fourteen years. After I became clean and sober, I came to the realization that I was a "dry drunk." This is someone who actually addresses his or her addiction—or at least the effects of that addiction—but never really understands the cause of the addiction and so keeps perpetuating the same situation over and over, even without an addictive substance being a factor. In other words, even though I abstained from alcohol, I still struggled with the emotional and psychological issues that caused my addiction to begin with. These negative effects continued to do damage to my psyche. That's why, even though I had stopped drinking, manifestations of anxiety, resentment, disappointment, and anger were still present in my life, causing key relationships to be worse than ever.

These negative emotions can often be hidden for quite some time. You might be able to hide them behind the mask of your job. You can conform and perform, and you can actually create an aptitude that becomes your identity. But there will come a time when that no longer works; the game changes. To really become the person you are meant to be requires a different set of skills, an entirely different set of circumstances. Finding yourself on unfamiliar ground will many times cause your unresolved issues to surface. Suddenly you're overwhelmed, and then you find yourself angry, anxious, and heading for disappointment, all because you haven't really understood the cause that creates the effect—you haven't dealt with unresolved events from the past.

"Neurons that fire together, wire together." This phrase was first coined by Donald Hebb, a Canadian neuropsychologist, in 1949. Your neural network is a system of connected neurons that transmit electrical patterns to send and receive information. What this means is that as you learn and experience something new, the neurons in your brain connect to create concepts by associative memory. Your ideas, thoughts, and feelings become your neural network.

When you are frequently angry, you are rewiring and reintegrating your neural network. When being angry, feeling like a victim, enduring suffering, and other negative emotional states show up on a daily basis, you are strengthening this pattern of connection in your neural network and creating a long-term relationship which becomes your identity.

I've devoted the last twenty-six years of my life to understanding brain chemistry—in particular the four main brainwave states of beta, alpha, theta, and delta.

Beta is the normal state of being awake consciously. In the beta state, we are alert, we reason, we think logically. These brainwaves can also lead to anxiety and stress.

A high-frequency beta state is typically what leads to anger and/or addiction—specifically unresolved issues—while lower-range frequencies produce clarity and creativity.

Alpha brain waves occur during meditation or when you're deeply relaxed. These brain waves are present at the base of your conscious awareness; this is where your intuition resides.

Theta and *delta* form the realm of your unconscious mind. In the theta state, you visualize, you create, you tap into inspiration. The delta state is the doorway to the universal, collective mind.

Your body doesn't operate well when you are in chaos, drama, overwhelm, or anxiety. Your body operates at its optimum performance when you are relaxed in the present, you are in the moment, and you are experiencing the alpha brainwave state.

The most relaxed state you can possibly be in is the delta state, where you can actually access the quantum field and the infinite source—this is a state of enlightenment. This means that you're so aware of what's going on that, through your highest level of consciousness, you can attract people or events in a synchronistic way, practically on command. All of us can create that kind of energy, but you can't do that in an overwhelmed, neurological state where serotonin levels drop and cortisol levels are elevated.

In this book we'll focus on how to move from a lower beta state full of anger and disappointment to the higher states of consciousness where peace and contentment flow.

Let's make sure we're clear about the definition of an unresolved issue. This is a past event you've either suppressed or forgotten about. Unresolved issues can stem from any multitude of situations you haven't really addressed. You might find yourself trying to overcome the situation, and so you think you are facing into it, but you are essentially only addressing the effect, not the cause. You lack the understanding of why you do what you do. Your favorite phrase becomes "I don't know."

- I don't know why I lost my composure.
- I don't know why I blew my cool.
- I don't know why this always happens to me.

Those three key words, "I don't know," keep you in a state called denial. If you are committed to realizing emotional and personal freedom, the road to success is paved with paying the price. You can put in the effort, but if your effort isn't directed in the right area, it typically will lead you to disappointment. That's why it's so important for you to understand the cause that creates the effect.

You might have strong business goals. But if you attempt to reach those goals while struggling with abandonment or rejection issues, you will sabotage your success by creating anxiety, overwhelm, and disappointment, which then will lead to anger directed at yourself. You won't be able to identify why you feel this way. The pattern goes like this:

- Events create feelings.
- Feelings become moods.
- Moods become an identity.

It's very common to create an identity of not understanding why you do what you do. This is called an *emotional addiction.* If you are dedicated and absolutely serious about changing the way you operate in your emotional self, throughout this book you'll receive fresh insights and gain a better understanding of the cause that creates the effect.

PART ONE
THE BACKSTORY

Anger is fuel. We feel it and we want to do something. Hit someone, break something, throw a fit, smash a fist into the wall, tell those bastards. But we are nice people, and what we do with our anger is stuff it, deny it, bury it, block it, hide it, lie about it, medicate it, muffle it, ignore it. We do everything but listen to it. Anger is meant to be listened to. Anger is a voice, a shout, a plea, a demand.... We are meant to use anger as a fuel to take the actions we need to move where our anger points us. With a little thought, we can usually translate the message that our anger is sending us.

JULIA CAMERON, *THE ARTIST'S WAY*

CHAPTER ONE
ANGER AFFECTS EVERYTHING

You have the best of intentions. You aspire to be a stellar spouse. An exceptional parent. A true leader. But day after day, situation after situation, you find yourself losing your cool, flying off the handle, letting someone have it…. Your spouse does or says something that irritates you. Your kids refuse to behave. In your work life it's just one problem after another. In your better moments you know the kind of person you are seeking to become. You have a vision of the life you know you are meant to live. But on a day-to-day basis, you are irritated, depressed, anxious, exhausted, frustrated, short-tempered, unhappy.

In a word, you're angry. You're someone who has angry outbursts on a regular basis. In fact, you might not remember when you didn't feel angry about something. From small, everyday irritations to big, seemingly insurmountable problems, the emotion you most often feel and the reaction you most regularly exhibit can be summed up in one word: anger.

That anger, unless you face into it and deal with it at its root causes, will be active beneath the surface. You may think it will just go away, you may think you can stuff it, but unfortunately this is not the case. Instead it will fester—like an open wound. Eventually your unresolved anger issues might cost you friends, jobs, or possibly your very freedom. No matter what, unresolved anger will absolutely cost you your peace of mind.

Before you can effectively deal with your anger and overcome it, it's necessary to examine the different kinds of anger and the causes of anger. We can break anger down into two main categories: normal and abnormal.

Normal Anger

Anger usually gets a bad rap in our society. We seldom think of anger as something positive or beneficial. However, there is a form of anger that is constructive and normal. Normal anger is healthy anger. It's a trigger that lets you know something is wrong; something is bothering you; there is something for you to deal with. Healthy anger can serve to protect you and your relationships. Anger can provide the motivation to stand up for yourself, or right a wrong, or fight against injustice. This kind of anger can lead to positive changes in your life or in society.

Angry feelings are just as valid as any other feelings; it's what you do with your feelings that counts. The emotion of anger has a wide range of expression; it encompasses everything from mild irritation to uncontrollable rage. With normal anger, however, you don't stay trapped in your angry feelings; instead you take productive action to address the situation. If the action doesn't work, you try something else. Eventually you are able to move on with your life.

Abnormal Anger

It's a different scenario with abnormal, or excessive, anger. This type of anger colors the way you see your world and everything in it. If you struggle with abnormal, unhealthy anger, you tend to see everything as a problem. Your mind constantly replays, over and over, what happened, who did what, who said this or that, and you find yourself in reaction mode, which only makes the situation worse. You ignore this fact, however, and continue to respond in ways that make it impossible for you to constructively address the issues. You are choosing—consciously or unconsciously—to hold onto your anger. Instead of moving on with your life, you are stuck...and angry.

This results in seeing life through a lens of anger. You might be on your daily commute, for example; it's a beautiful, sunny day, but rather than enjoying music on the radio and reflecting on what your day might hold, you focus on the driver who just cut you off in traffic. Anger colors the rest of your day, and your reality reflects that negative perspective. At lunch the server gets your order wrong. Your boss makes demands that you perceive as unreasonable. Your commute home is fraught with red lights and frustrating drivers. You arrive home tired and irritable—and the rest of the evening is downhill from there.

Normal anger shows up periodically, and then it's gone. With abnormal anger, you find yourself erupting in angry outbursts frequently, and you stay angry for a long time. And it's not only others who receive the brunt of your anger. You turn that anger inward on yourself, too, which leads to a host of unhealthy behaviors—from binge drinking to physical violence and dangerous, out-of-control episodes. Anger now has you in its grip; it has become an obsession. And the more you obsess about what makes you angry, the angrier you get.

Let's take a look at all the areas abnormal anger touches.

Your Health

Anger is detrimental to your health, as much of a hazard as smoking or eating too much sugar. It affects your blood pressure and causes tension within your body. It can cause accidents, and the reality is that it can take years off your life.

When you get angry, your heart rate increases, along with cortisol (the stress hormone) levels. Your muscles tense up, your digestive processes are comprised, and your brain chemistry is negatively altered. Studies have shown that habitually angry individuals tend to have more calcium deposits in their coronary arteries, putting them at a higher risk for heart attacks. Suppressing your anger isn't the answer, either—new studies show that this can even triple your chances of having a heart attack.

Over time your immune system is weakened, and this can lead to a variety of other health problems such as headaches, insomnia, high blood pressure, skin problems (such as eczema), or stroke. There's no getting around the fact that your emotional health is intricately tied to your physical health. We'll explore this in more depth in later chapters.

Your Wealth

You might not initially think that anger has anything to do with a person's wealth. However, it's one of the key internal obstacles to financial success. Anger repels wealth. Bitterness and anger are poisonous and in direct opposition to building wealth and prosperity.

When it comes right down to it, anger is costly—it's a very expensive habit. You may do harm to yourself or others, resulting in medical bills or lawsuits. You might go on a rampage that destroys your possessions or your neighbor's property. What about accidents that result from driving recklessly while your emotions were out of control? Maybe your anger will destroy your marriage—costly emotionally, but also very expensive in terms of attorney fees and possibly child support.

Anger leads to poor decisions regarding money: impulsive spending, inability to live within your means, rash business decisions, and so on. When you struggle with unresolved anger, you tend to feel pessimistic, and this can have an effect on your financial decisions. When you're caught up in anger, you become careless with your thoughts; irrational anger goes hand in hand with irrational, poorly executed decisions.

If you're angry there's a high probability you will alienate people from your circle of influence. When you're angry, resentful, hostile, or hateful, you send a mixed message to people that says, "Come near me and violate me," or "Allow me to violate you." That kind of energy typically isn't conducive to collaboration or creating results—whether in life or in business.

However, anger is not a black-and-white situation, because there are angry people who do have various degrees of success. There are successful people who channel their anger into addictions, thus sabotaging themselves. Individuals might have different degrees of success, but the fact remains: Anger is an energy that is ineffective long-term when it comes to achievement because it's exhausting, it's overwhelming, and it alienates good people from your circle of influence. It puts others in a position where they are uncomfortable around you. Anger is not conducive to any kind of prosperity.

Your Relationships

Habitual anger is detrimental to your relationships with those you love the most. Instead of drawing your family members to you, you push them away. They might continue to love you from a distance—but anger slams the door on meaningful conversation and enjoyable activities you could otherwise share with them.

If you don't think your anger affects those closest to you, think again. What do you think your spouse would say about how he or she sees you?

There's also the whole issue of physical abuse. If there are any episodes of violent behavior going on, your struggle with anger is a serious one. And while you might not resort to physical abuse, if you often find yourself screaming or yelling or hurling insults, if you're into the shame game or the blame game, the issue of anger is not a minor one in your life.

How about your relationships with your extended family? Are there relatives you haven't spoken to for years due to some unresolved issue? Long-term, habitual anger can alienate families and affect multiple generations.

Angry individuals tend not to be very popular. They repel others, hold grudges, and write people off until they find themselves isolated and alone.

Your Personality

When you are habitually angry, it affects you in ways you might not realize. You might find yourself becoming paranoid, questioning others' motives, always suspicious of those around you. Angry individuals often resort to sarcasm and scathing remarks, leading to mean-spiritedness. Anger leads to apathy, irresponsible behavior, and other self-defeating behaviors.

Those who are habitually angry live with guilt and shame, which occur in those moments when they realize how they've hurt those around them once again. Even if you think of yourself as a person with strong values, when you're throwing an angry fit, all that goes out the window, and in its place unwanted emotions entrench themselves in your psyche: hate, impatience, meanness, and other unpleasant emotions. Aside from turning you into someone even you don't want to be around, habitual anger can rob your life of joy and fulfillment, leaving only emptiness and a sense of futility.

The Many Faces of Anger

How does anger show up in your life? Here are three

telltale signs that can reveal the unresolved anger in your life and explain why you are so often disgruntled and unhappy.

You feel unappreciated. No matter how hard you try, you can't seem to please those around you. You work long hours, you make sacrifices, but those you sacrifice for don't seem to respect you or even recognize or appreciate all you've done for them. At work you put in extra hours, but your boss fails to affirm you or compensate you for the extra effort you expend on his behalf.

Life feels like a battle. When you look around, others don't seem to struggle the way that you do. They seem to float effortlessly through their days, while you seemingly are slogging through mud. People seem like adversaries; you must constantly be on your guard or defending your position.

Everyone else seems to be happier than you are. Especially with the advent of social media, it's easy to feel that everyone else has an amazing life with no challenges or heartaches. You, on the other hand, can never seem to get ahead or enjoy the good things in life. For you life is one long struggle with no end in sight, and it doesn't seem fair.

But Why?

Why would you—or anyone else, for that matter—want to live this way? The fact that you are reading this book reveals that you really don't want to live like this. You don't want to be an angry, impatient person. However, the fact of the matter is that you are the only one who can really do something to change this reality.

Picking up a book like this is a good start. Overcoming habitual anger requires brutal honesty. It takes courage to admit that you're not a poor, innocent victim. You have to stop lying to yourself and admit that you have become a person who is full of anger. Being a rageaholic might have become your identity. Remember, an identity is created by moods, which are created by feelings. You are not actually a rageaholic, but you have taken on the identity of an angry person. Once you understand the cause behind the effect, you can let go of identities that no longer serve you.

Admitting the truth is the first step. You will always have challenges, but how you deal with those challenges is what is important. Anger, guilt, shame, and resentment are all by-products of events and your perception of the events that have shaped your identity. As you address the feelings that have created your emotions, you will begin to let go of the events you have stuffed. To recover is a one-day-at-a-time process to release your anger and guilt, express your feelings openly, and not worry about the future.

In the rest of this book, I'll present ways you can do this once and for all. But first let's examine the factors that have created this situation. In the next chapter we'll take a look at why you are so angry.

Ask Yourself

1. *How has my anger affected those around me?*

2. *How has my anger affected me?*

3. *How might angry reactions have an impact on my income?*

CHAPTER TWO
THE ROOTS OF ANGER

You've taken a big step by facing into your abnormal anger. Self-awareness is key. But before you can let go of anger and move into a relaxed, peaceful state, it's important to understand the causes behind the effects. Knowing how you got so angry is vital for you to change this situation.

Where does anger begin? Anger begins with an event. The more you understand the events that have shaped your feelings, the more you will start to let go of this false statement: "My whole childhood was a blur; I don't remember anything." You do remember. You simply have chosen not to remember. You have not forgotten anything.

If you examine the families of those who struggle with unresolved anger, you'll find that they were raised by angry mothers, fathers, grandmothers, grandfathers, aunts, uncles. As children they were conditioned to react in anger because that's what they observed and absorbed their circle of influence doing. Because they never experienced anything else, they learned to assume that such behavior was normal.

We learn how to act from those who raise us. If a key adult in your life habitually blew up at the slightest provocation, you most likely learned to model that same behavior, even though as a child you recoiled from it. If you saw your father disrespecting others, there's a high probability that you will treat others with disrespect, too. Often those who are convicted of sexual abuse crimes reveal that they themselves were sexually abused as children.

If your father was given to frequent rages, there's a good chance your mother had her own issues with anger. She may have stuffed her anger, so it was nowhere near as overt as your father's, but unresolved anger absolutely was part of her identity. What this meant for you as a child is that you were surrounded by anger. You also were not able to discern between healthy and unhealthy anger.

Does this mean that you require therapy, a coach, or a mentor? Not necessarily. It does require being candid, being objective, being real, being genuine, being authentic, and being able to face what you have been through courageously, without feeling like a victim.

Many anger addicts develop a victim mentality. Of course, anger addicts do not like to be called victims. It makes them angrier. Granted, it does not take a lot to spark more anger in someone who is angry all the time. What happens when you are angry all the time?

- You experience road rage.
- You seek out people to violate you.
- You set up people to disappoint you.
- You go out of your way to create a confrontational situation.
- You are addicted to conflict.

Conflict creates that edgy edge. You are just waiting for someone to irritate you, violate you, make you mad, cut you off in traffic, hang up on you—anything so you can feel rejected, abandoned, neglected, overwhelmed, and unorganized, which then gives you the opportunity to completely move into a state of unresolved anger.

You're traveling and your flight is canceled. Full of unresolved anger, you react. "I knew this would happen to me. I had a first-class ticket. I knew it was too good to be true. I knew this flight would be canceled." You're primed to "go off" on the first person that crosses your path. That was me, the nuclear reactor. I spent fourteen years of my life proving I was right, and eventually I ended up very broke and very broken.

Ronald T. Potter-Efron wrote a book that changed my life called *Angry All the Time*. In that book he says:

> *Angry people come from angry families. The single most common cause of severe anger is an angry home. Kids learn how angry they should be from their parents. They learn when to get angry. And how. And how much. It's called modeling.*[3]

How many of you can relate? And while as children we may not have liked the behavior we saw our parents and caregivers model, we were like little sponges, absorbing those toxic outbursts and learning to respond the very same way.

Three Destructive Beliefs of Angry Families

While each family situation is unique, angry families share some similar traits. Here are three beliefs they typically have in common:[4]

Being angry is normal. While the proper use of anger lets us know that something is amiss, in angry families it is so habitual that the warning signs are diffused. Someone is always angry about something—and everyone thinks this is perfectly normal behavior.

No one listens until someone gets angry. In this situation, the only way to get anyone's attention is to lash out in anger. It's the only way parents feel their kids will listen and obey. It's the only way kids think they can get what they want. This leads to becoming a family of rageaholics.

Problems are solved with anger. The mistake here is that no one realizes that "anger is a signal, not a solution." Anger can alert you to the fact that there is some kind of a problem. But what angry families fail to realize is that anger doesn't solve anything. In fact, overreacting in anger only creates more problems.

The people we grow up with typically will create much of the anger we carry with us into adulthood, but it's important to realize that anger is not hereditary. There is no link to the DNA of anger. Anger is not genetic. Anger is based on cause and effect. For every effect, there is an underlying cause that creates a feeling, a mood, or an identity, and anger is a key emotion that affects a large percentage of the population.

When you hold onto your anger and resentment, you

are giving power to the situations where you felt rejection, abandonment, violation, and disappointment. Letting go and forgiving allows you to begin the healing process. Holding on keeps you a victim and keeps you stuck, while letting go and forgiving liberates you and frees you from past unresolved events that keep you angry.

If you didn't grow up in an angry family, but you still find yourself angry all the time, there are several situations that can lead to this.

Unresolved Issues

Anger typically stems from events, because it is events that shape our beliefs. It is the perception of an event that creates an emotional state. If anger is one of your states, you most likely will have challenges connecting with people. All of the following expressions of anger refer to unresolved issues that we are somehow holding onto, even though we may not be consciously aware of those issues:

- road rage
- being angry all the time
- unresolved anger
- overt anger
- repressed anger

An unresolved issue typically means that we do not remember it. We stuff it. Something upsetting happened to us at some point in our past, and as adults we now say, "My childhood was a blur; I really do not remember my childhood." Maybe you grew up in a dysfunctional household with adults who struggled with addictions. Or perhaps you grew up feeling that you had to be careful not to upset your parents or siblings or grandparents. These situations can lead to unresolved anger in adulthood, whether that anger is expressed passively or aggressively. Some situations that create unresolved issues include:

- growing up in an unpredictable environment
- being raised by a passive-aggressive parent, grandparent, or other caregiver
- experiencing a passive-aggressive sibling, neighbor, or other individual in your circle of influence
- being bullied or picked on at the playground by your classmates
- being teased or made fun of by your playmates

In my coaching practice, I ask my clients to identify the cause of a particular situation, and many of them are only able to state the effect over and over. I assist them to realize that what they are describing is a series of events that have shaped their feelings. The way you perceive an event creates your feelings, your moods, your very identity. *The unresolved issues you hold onto form your neurological network.* This is a very important principle.

Understanding Cause and Effect

Your subconscious has a memory of every event that has ever happened to you. When you were six years old walking down the street and a car splashed mud on you, and you went home and your mother got very angry at you for getting your clothes dirty, your subconscious remembers that even though you may have forgotten it in your conscious mind. It is now in your unconscious.

You may say, "I don't remember what happened in my past," but that would have been an event that could have an effect on you, especially if you got punished. So if you were someone who has gotten in trouble—and getting in trouble is now part of your identity—or you're worried about being in trouble, that has now become an anxiety. Anxieties are effects, not causes. All anxieties are direct reflections of events that shaped your feelings. Feelings become moods, moods become identities, and identities become part of who you are. That's why, if you are seeking change, it's vital to understand the cause that creates the effect of why you do what you do. Unless you understand why you do what you do, you'll continue to do that which is familiar.

If you are serious about changing and transforming, letting go is the key to being prosperous, spiritual, available, genuine, authentic, and in the present. But in order to let go, you have to know what to let go of. Letting go is a surrendering technique: You're not surrendering out of weakness; you're actually surrendering from your power.

The events that have shaped your feelings happened

in your childhood, your adolescence, your teenage years—they happened yesterday, today, last week. And whenever they've happened, they created in you a feeling, a mood, and finally an identity.

A lot of our anxiety is based on past events—specifically as children growing up if we were not given the proper tools, techniques, guidance, mentoring, or therapy to learn to let go. Letting go is a decision, and it's also a process.

When you hold onto that which you don't understand, and when what you don't understand is anger, then there's a high probability that you are going to get or be angry all the time in a multitude of situations.

Events shape our feelings. There are events from your past that created the anger you struggle with today. You may have been violated; you may have been abused; you may have been neglected. You may not have been able to please the people around you. You may have grown up with passive-aggressive angry personalities in your circle of influence. The more you understand the cause that creates the effect, the better the opportunity and the awareness for you to let go of the events that shaped your feelings.

If you're serious about letting go of anger, then it's important that you learn to forgive and not hold other people responsible for your feelings today. When you separate your feelings from events that no longer serve you, you no longer have the mind/body connection to the event that shaped your identity of anger and anxiety.

To understand cause and effect, you must

understand the events that shaped the feelings. If you are overwhelmed, that's an effect. If you have low self-esteem, that's an effect, not a cause. If you are in guilt or shame, that's an effect—that's an emotion; it's not a cause. If you are overwhelmed, if you are anxious, if you are unorganized, these are all effects. Effects are based on causes. The more you understand the cause that creates the effect, the more awareness you will have, and the better chance you'll have of letting go of the control that keeps you overwhelmed in control.

Sexual or Physical Abuse

One of the most common unresolved issues affecting a large part of the population is being personally violated. Three out of five women have been sexually molested. Two out of five men have been molested. That means half of the population right there. When these violations occur we typically live in silent shame. We endure silent guilt. We hold onto those events, and they then create our neurological network, which becomes a feeling, a mood, and an identity.

Those who have been physically violated may have survived, but they are badly damaged. They can't seem to forget the abuse or put it behind them so they can get on with their lives. Often abuse victims will remember every episode, every time they were struck, every single humiliation—and they remember now with anger instead of the terror they felt as children. They might harbor thoughts of revenge or retaliation toward the abuser.

And although the victims of abuse recoil at the very

thought of what they endured, all too often they themselves become abusers. Maybe a husband uses physical abuse to deal with his wife. Or a mother resorts to physical punishment with her child. In cases like these, the abusers oftentimes say they can't seem to control themselves, even though they are ashamed and even horrified by their behavior. Filled with bitterness and resentment, they end up continuing the cycle of abuse.

Those who have been sexually abused often keep their rage buried deep within for years. The very memory of the abuse might be repressed so fully that it's as though it never happened. But at some point in their adult life, they can no longer stuff this memory and it suddenly surfaces. This begins the process of facing the reality of the violation and dealing with all the effects that this cause has created in their life. It can be a lengthy and painful journey, but for those who have been abused, awareness and honesty open the door to authentic healing.

Addictions

Addictions stem from unresolved issues. Unresolved anger is one of the most common causes of addiction. It is very typical for an angry individual (whether he or she recognizes the anger or not) to use alcohol, drugs, food, compulsive spending, gambling, anorexia, bulimia, or being in debt to take the edge off. I call this the "edgy edge." Another word for it is *angst*—A-N-G-S-T—which is a feeling of deep anxiety or dread about the world in general.

Being addicted keeps you lying to yourself, with a loss of integrity; it keeps you overwhelmed and perpetuates a low self-esteem that results in attracting the same situations over and over, causing you to feel continually disappointed.

No matter what sort of exterior outer substance you turn to in order to take that edge off, your body doesn't lie. Back in the 80s, I thought I knew how many shots of courage (i.e., Dewars Scotch) it took to consume in order to drink my pain away. I learned the hard way: There is no amount of alcohol or drugs that can ever take away that kind of discomfort. A body in pain stays in pain.

Pain creates anxiety. Anxiety creates disorganization. Disorganization leads to chaos and unnecessary drama. Pain, anxiety, and disorganization all combine to create unresolved issues.

Your addictions are a direct reflection of your perception of events that left you feeling violated, rejected, abandoned, and overwhelmed. Holding onto these events creates guilt, shame, and unresolved anger, often leading to an overwhelming desire to stuff your feelings with food, alcohol, drugs, compulsive spending, gambling, and other unhealthy situations. When you become aware and understand the cause that creates the effect, you have a better opportunity to let go of the control that controls you.

I realized after several years of recovery that I was a *dry drunk*. I had addressed the effect of my alcohol addiction, but I never addressed the cause that created that effect. I became a dry addict. I was sober, but I still had not addressed the unresolved issues that led to my addiction in the first place.

Studies have shown that there is a strong correlation

between issues with alcohol and issues with anger; they seem to go hand in hand. Alcohol increases aggressive behavior in individuals with aggressive personality traits to begin with. Impulsive, spontaneous types are especially susceptible. Alcohol and anger are a toxic mix.

Shame

Many individuals walk around this planet in silent shame. They are ashamed of *themselves*—not for something they did, but for who they *are*. They feel bad about themselves; they feel that *they* are bad. If you suffer from shame, you might find yourself thinking about yourself this way:

I'll never be good enough.

I'm not lovable.

I don't fit in.

I don't deserve to be alive.

What is the relationship between shame and anger? Many people feel shame when they get angry. They have been taught that all anger is inappropriate, so they strive to never be angry. And when they do become angry, they feel guilty and ashamed.

Shame can also lead to becoming angry at yourself. Those with habitual shame are always frustrated and end up with a large amount of self-hatred. Nothing they do is ever good enough. And while this shame is directed inside, it also can result in being quick to shame others. All this shame eventually leads to rage.

If you went through a situation where you were traumatized, picked on, molested, abandoned, or neglected, if you grew up on the wrong side of the tracks, if you are a slow learner—your whole body language can give off a series of emotions that telegraph to others the fact that you've been victimized, that you are struggling, that you live in shame.

Struggling is not noble. Struggling is exhausting and only leads to more addictions and eventually hitting rock bottom.

Self-Assertiveness

If you carry these types of feelings into adulthood, in effect you have carried the past into the present, and you'll have challenges asking for what you deserve. You're going to have a difficult time asking for a commitment, whether it's in a business situation or in your personal life. Instead of being direct and transparent, you'll find it difficult to articulate what you desire. You'll often live with a very vague state of emotions which leads to you not wanting to push people, not wanting to bother people, and not feeling comfortable asserting yourself.

One of the biggest effects of worry, guilt, and shame is conflict avoidance. No matter what the outcome you are seeking to create, it's easy to fabricate stories about the outcome so you can avoid the conflict. You might tell yourself, "Oh, I don't like conflict; I don't like confrontation." The reality is that you have an issue with asking for what you deserve.

Conflict isn't always physical. When you're interacting

with others, it's typically a non-physical experience. You aren't pushing anyone around physically. You should be able to communicate clearly, collaborate openly, and ask honest questions of those with whom you come in contact.

You should be able to engage in small talk, fact-finding, and rapport building, and thus create emotional experiences that are favorable to sustaining long-term, meaningful relationships.

Self-Talk

But what if your self-talk goes something like this?

> I'm not good enough because of events from my past. I'm not separated from those past events. Those past events define me. What happened in the past has created my identity. I can't really talk to certain people because I'm just not that good. They're up there; I'm just little old me down here. I'm from the wrong side of the tracks. I'm tiptoeing quietly through life just trying to get by.

Unfortunately this is common self-talk for many people, and it's a key reason for self-sabotage.

Your self-talk is the fundamental key for either letting go or staying where you are. If your self-talk is not conducive to an emotional state that results in healthy self-esteem, then you'll be in an unhealthy state full of mixed messages. These mixed messages can be both verbal and nonverbal. They wreak havoc on your own self-perception, and they can have negative consequences for your relationships, whether business or personal.

Please show up and abandon me...reject me... violate me...leave me...disappoint me.

Let's have a relationship that doesn't work out so I can prove myself right. See, I knew that wouldn't work.

Another phenomenon you'll experience if you live in guilt and shame—whether it's conscious or unconscious—is that you shut out certain personalities. I've coached many entrepreneurs who weren't able to connect with A-type personalities or highly successful individuals because they told themselves a story about these types, and it's relatively black-and-white. They had a preconceived idea that high-powered individuals might hurt them or pick on them—and absolutely they would never want to partner with them.

When conflict is a way of life, you will go to extremes to create the events and attract people to fulfill your biochemical addiction to conflict. Conflict represents the past events of being violated, traumatized, rejected, and abandoned. If you are angry all the time, live in disappointment, and create dramatic scenes to prove you are right, you have a conflict consciousness.

Anger and conflict do not serve you; they alienate the very people you seek to attract. The lack of comfort you feel manifests itself out in the world, and this kind of "neural net" then only allows you to attract other codependents, other people who also live in guilt and shame.

Essentially you have a very small "law of the lid." This means that your ability to lead determines your level of effectiveness. When you raise your "lid" (your leadership ability), you become increasingly effective in the marketplace (and in all areas of life). A small lid leads to failure and disappointment, the fundamental beliefs you created to begin with. You'll never attract more than what you unconsciously believe you're capable of attracting.

Has Anger Become Your Identity?

Unresolved anger can form a person's identity. People used to say to me, "Wow, you look really angry." Do you know what that would do? That would make me even angrier. People would point out my anger, and I would want to fly into a rage. I wore my anger on my sleeve as though it were a badge of honor—or at least that is what my ego led me to believe. I had a colossal chip on my shoulder. It would totally upset me when people pointed out how angry I was. I was someone who was angry all the time—it had become my identity, and I no longer saw it as anything but normal.

No one becomes an angry individual overnight. Understanding the roots of your anger and facing into what anger has created in your life is the beginning of becoming healthy. In future chapters, I'll provide some proven strategies for letting go of toxic anger and becoming the peaceful, fulfilled person you know you are meant to be.

Ask Yourself

1. *Where did my anger begin? Were there angry role models in my life? How did they model habitual anger for me?*

2. *Do I see a correlation between any physical or emotional issues and my struggle with anger?*

3. *In addition to anger, do I struggle with shame? How does this manifest itself in my life?*

CHAPTER THREE
WHY ANGER IS HARD TO SHAKE

When was the last time you truly felt full of happiness, gratitude, and peace? If you have unresolved anger issues, this is typically a rare state for you.

Unresolved anger creates a situation where many people bounce between the negative emotions of anger and fear. If this is your experience, you typically look for quick fixes that might ease episodes of blind rage and alleviate anxious thoughts. But temporary fixes don't address the root cause of your anger, which only continues to get worse.

Resentment, anger, and fear are all connected, and this creates a vicious cycle. Those who haven't dealt with anger from past events find themselves trapped in an endless loop of being afraid of the future, angry in the present, and filled with resentment over the past.

We are conditioned to repress our anger, which creates resentment when held onto. Many of us carry unresolved anger from past violations involving people who have used guilt to control us.

One of the reasons anger and resentment are so hard to shake is that there is so much bad advice out there on how to deal with them. Someone close to you might tell you to "just get over it." Or you might hear, "What's past is past. Forget it and move on." But ignoring accumulated anger from past events unequivocally doesn't work.

Your perception of what happens to you is what starts to create your identity. If you are able to let go of a particular event, you are able to separate yourself from it, and the event does not own you. When you take ownership of your feelings, you begin to have command of your feelings. You let go of the control that keeps you out of control, feeling overwhelmed and addicted, or feeling unorganized. That's when you start to change; you start to move into recovery. Remember, if you continue to do the same things over and over, you will create the same effects.

All effects are direct reflections of causes. And causes are direct reflections of events. If you grew up with an adult who had a passive-aggressive personality, you probably learned that you couldn't please that person. You may have concluded that you couldn't please *anyone*. If you were emotionally or physically abused, there is a high probability that those experiences have become a part of your neurology, which means that you've learned to live in a state of fight-or-flight. You flinch; you check out; you say "um" a lot; you don't want to make a mistake.

The fight-or-flight response is also known as the acute stress response. It is a term first coined in the 1920s to describe the way animals react to threats. In humans, when presented with an event that threatens or frightens us, we experience a strong physical desire to escape, even when there is nothing physically threatening about the event. For instance, you might be in a business meeting when suddenly your boss accuses you of not following through on something that you know was someone else's responsibility. You can feel anger building inside of you, and you have a strong desire to flee the room. Your life is not in danger, but you still experience a physical desire to escape.

Past Events Do Not Equal Present Feelings

I'm here to tell you that past events do not have to equal present feelings. But when a past event ends up stored in your psyche, there is a high probability that some kind of outlet is going to be required to neutralize those feelings you continue to stuff. That outlet might be food; it might be an addiction; it might be angry outbursts. This only causes you to hold onto those past events.

Anger stems from fear. When you get angry, it means that someone or something has threatened you, and this threat causes you to feel afraid. You might encounter a situation you don't feel able to address with confidence. Anger then becomes an attempt to "intimidate your opponent," as David R. Hawkins mentions in his book, *Letting Go*.[5] This type of anger stems from weakness; you are not coming from a place of strength. You feel unequal to the situation. Only truly surrendered individuals can express anger, and this is because they *choose* to be angry; they are not forced to use anger to handle a situation.

You cannot change what you continue to deny. Letting go is the decision to no longer give significance or feelings to past events that do not serve you. When you let go, you are letting go of the emotions based on past events that have created an identity. Letting go is liberating and allows you to move on from what has kept you disappointed, addicted, and overwhelmed. Letting go is a decision that allows you to free yourself from events, people, and situations that have kept you from being your best self.

What's done is done. It's water under the bridge; it's history. Why do we so often find ourselves stuck reliving the past, not able to live fully in the present? Why can't we let go? What keeps us angry?

Five Reasons You Stay Angry

Let's take a look at the reasons people can't seem to shake anger and move on. I've identified five main reasons, but you might come up with others. The interesting thing—and this is important to note—is that habitual anger is serving you in some way. You might not be conscious of this, but if you really had no use for your anger, you'd drop it immediately.

You are seeking control. Whether it is in your marriage, or at your place of employment, or in your social circle—you want to be in charge. You don't want anyone else telling you what to do, how to act, or where to go. Because of faulty role models or negative events you've experienced, somewhere along the line you learned that yelling or threatening others created the opportunity to get your own way. For the most part it has worked for you—well, at least for a while…at least in some situations. The trouble here is that it's a very immature way to act; it's the adult version of throwing a tantrum. Anger might get someone to do what you insist, but there are so many other, more positive ways to influence others.

You are a victim. You tell yourself it's not your fault. The reason you're so angry is someone else's fault. You'd be happy and serene if only you didn't have to put up with such ignorant, irritating people. You have a right to be angry—how else could you be expected to respond to such behavior?

Or perhaps you feel like a martyr. You're doing the lion's share of the work. You're sacrificing your time and energy for someone, and he or she doesn't seem to recognize it. You certainly don't receive gratitude or appreciation for all you do. How else are you supposed to feel but angry?

If you feel like a victim, you choose not to take risks. You stay in a place of inaction, and this way you avoid confrontation and stay powerless. You see others as out to get you, so you become defensive and self-absorbed. You have a "poor me" attitude, and you see others as better than you. A victim has very little self-confidence and takes little or no initiative.

If you see yourself in these descriptions, it's time to take a step back and look at things objectively. The bottom line here is that you have relinquished responsibility for your own actions. You're playing the blame game, and that's a game you'll never win. Nothing will ever change until you recognize that you are the only one who can do something about you and your feelings.

You have poor self-talk. In every walk of life, it's important to continually improve your communication skills with others. Whether you're a business owner, a parent, a teacher, or an employee, being able to articulate your ideas and feelings clearly and honestly is an important skill to cultivate. However, by far the most important person you communicate with is *you*. Self-talk—the way you communicate with yourself—determines the way you communicate with others. Take a moment and think about how you communicate with yourself.

- Do you get frustrated with yourself?
- Do you judge yourself?
- Can you receive a compliment?
- Do you feel unworthy?
- Do you deserve success?

Your unconscious mind does not separate fact from fiction. It will do exactly what you teach or train it to do. That's the way it's been conditioned. If your self-talk is below par, you'll continue to do the same things over and over, and no matter how promising situations look at the outset, you'll end up disappointed again.

The books you read, the audios you listen to, and the people you surround yourself with all influence the way you think and the way you talk to yourself. Start studying successful, prosperous, healthy individuals; watch what they do. Listen to the way they speak. You'll begin to let go of limiting thoughts and doubts. As you gradually learn to upgrade your self-talk, this will become a new and powerful habit, and new patterns will emerge in your life.

You are "feelings resistant." You are not able or willing to express your emotions. Your anger is a mask that protects you from allowing yourself to feel deeply.

Somehow you've gotten the idea that feelings are negative, a sign of weakness. In your mind anger seems powerful, while expressing sadness or even deep joy appear weak and even dangerous. Your anger has become so much a part of you that it actually feels safe.

Your anger acts as a barrier between you and the rest of the world. While your anger protects you from people and situations that might hurt you, it also keeps you from living life to the fullest. It might protect you from pain, but it also prevents you from experiencing joy and peace—and most importantly, love. People who are angry all the time are living a sub-human existence.

What would happen if you let go of your anger? You might find yourself hurt or abandoned or betrayed, at least for a time. But you just might find yourself fully alive, in love with life and experiencing the richness of intimacy.

You are addicted to anger. Just as a person becomes addicted to drugs or alcohol, you can become addicted to being angry. At first glance this seems like a strange addiction. With drugs or alcohol, people usually enjoy the way they feel, at least initially. But who enjoys being angry?

Well…you do. There is a certain adrenaline rush that accompanies angry outbursts that is powerful—and addictive. It's not so much that you *like* being angry—in fact, you might not feel good at all; you might feel awful and ashamed of yourself—but the powerful sensation, the strong feeling, is intense, actually exciting in a way.

The author of *Angry All the Time* refers to this as "excited misery." He says:

A lot of people stay angry because they don't want to give up the intensity of feeling that it provides.... The reason they stay angry is so they can keep getting high. Some very angry people are emotional junkies. They have become emotionally addicted to their anger. *They may tell you they don't like it, and that may be true. But they* need *it. And that's why it's so hard for them to let go of their anger.*[6]

This "anger rush" is so addictive because at least when you're angry, you feel alive. The blood is coursing through your veins; you experience a surge of energy. When the anger subsides, life goes back to being dull, boring, flat. You've become emotionally dependent on your anger.

Breaking the Cycle

How can you break this cycle? You must overcome the events that shape those feelings. This requires that you address why you do what you do. It starts with taking a good look at your family because this is where a lot of your behaviors were created. When you start to address why you do what you do, it's important to do it objectively—without blaming people from your past, without being so judgmental you can't possibly move into any state of ease or prosperity—and you must learn to do it one day at a time.

As you study the five reasons people stay in their

anger, think about the one or two you struggle with the most. That's where you want to focus your energy. As you start to make changes, you will see your life transform in remarkable ways.

One way to start is to create some reasons to succeed, reasons to let go of your anger identity. Develop the awareness that your past does not equal your future—affirm this daily. Really go into detail about your ideal life. Without the burden of anger weighing you down, what would your future look like? What might you be able to accomplish? What would your relationships look like? What about your finances? Think about your ideal day. Describe it in detail. The clearer you are about this, the better chance you have of making it a reality. This is your new game plan.

Grab your notebook or journal and write some affirmations for yourself. Use the present tense and be specific. Here are some examples to get you started:

Anger is no longer my identity.

My past does not equal my future.

I am not afraid to show my emotions.

I am letting go of my anger one day at a time.

I am in control of my reactions.

Give yourself the space to develop these new habits, this new identity. Don't be too hard on yourself—you are human. As you develop a new mindset, you might find yourself full of regret over the time you've wasted being

WHY ANGER IS HARD TO SHAKE

angry and miserable. Regret paralyzes you; you'll find yourself right back living in the past instead of living in the solution. Don't fall into this trap.

I'll close this chapter with the Serenity Prayer. This prayer has brought me many moments of peace and calmness, and it's very appropriate to overcoming anger and dealing with the pain of regret.

God, grant me the serenity to accept the things I cannot change, the courage to change the things I can, and the wisdom to know the difference.

Ask Yourself

1. *Describe the type of anger you struggle with. Why is your anger so hard to shake?*

2. *List the top three reasons for letting go of anger in your life.*

3. *For the next week, pray the Serenity Prayer each morning. At the end of the day, note in your journal the difference this has made in your day.*

PART TWO
THE EFFECTS OF ANGER

At the moment you become angry, you tend to believe
that your misery has been created by another person.
You blame him or her for all your suffering. But by
looking deeply, you may realize that the seed of anger
in you is the main cause of your suffering. Many other
people, confronted with the same situation, would not
get angry like you. They hear the same words, they see
the same situation, and yet they are able to stay calm and
not be carried away. Why do you get angry so easily?
You may get angry very easily because your seed of anger
is too strong. And because you have not practiced the
methods for taking good care of your anger, the seed of
anger has been watered too often in the past.

THICH NHAT HANH, *ANGER*

CHAPTER FOUR
FROM ANGER TO ADDICTION

Now that we've identified the issue of anger, examined the roots of anger, and looked at why anger is so difficult to overcome, we'll focus our attention on some of the effects of anger. In this chapter we'll cover a big one: how anger leads to various addictions.

Those who are habitually angry are prime candidates for addiction. The accumulation of angry feelings, thoughts, words, actions, and reactions can lead to seeking relief from all that negativity in drugs or alcohol (or even food, shopping, the Internet, and so on).

Too often this turns into abusing drugs or alcohol, and the result is a full-blown addiction. Instead of helping to alleviate anger, addiction just makes it worse and leads to a new set of problems. Addiction quite often destroys families, jobs, relationships, as well as one's health and financial well-being.

Alcohol Addiction

Alcohol addiction is the most common type of drug abuse. Instead of calming an angry individual down, it often has the opposite effect and escalates anger's intensity to the point of violence toward oneself and others. Alcohol is typically a factor in all sorts of crime and the cause of many accidents. From domestic abuse to murder and rape and even suicide, the alcohol factor cannot be overlooked or minimized. How do you know if you're abusing alcohol? Here are some questions to ask yourself:

- Do I ever drive after I've had a few drinks?
- Have I ever sustained an injury while drinking?
- Have I ever engaged in binge drinking?
- Do I feel a strong need to drink?
- Do I ever drink more than I intend to?
- Has drinking affected my health?
- Has alcohol cost me any relationships?
- Have I ever tried to quit drinking but couldn't?
- Does my drinking affect my family life?
- Has a hangover ever kept me from going to work?

If you habitually drink too much, you might have an addiction to alcohol. I'll share my own story. I'm a recovering alcoholic and drug addict. Between the ages of eighteen and thirty-two, I spent my life dosing myself with anything and everything to dull my pain and stuff my anger.

My addictions led to me being arrested five times. At one point I was drinking a gallon of vodka a day. My drinking escalated to the point that I experienced delirium tremors. Very early in my drinking career, I started to experience blackouts. I was very proud of how much I could drink; I used to walk around bragging that no one could drink me under the table. That was not true, however, because I ended up under the table many times during those blackouts. And yes, I was the type of drinker who would look across the bar and notice that someone had left half a beer or half a shot. When no one was looking, I would finish it, just to take the edge off, that edgy edge. No matter what, though, I could never drink my pain and anger away.

No one starts out wanting to become an alcoholic or a drug addict. It usually begins with just a drink or two socially. A glass of wine or a couple of beers lowers your inhibitions, making you feel relaxed. Drinking makes it easier to interact with others socially. However, no longer "uptight," drinkers can become rowdy and impulsive, leading to behaviors they would normally avoid. Alcohol makes it easier to laugh and have fun, but it also makes it easier for someone to get angry and lash out.

Once a pattern of drinking is in place, it is difficult to regain control. If you have an addictive personality, it's probable that you will require professional help to overcome your addiction. This is due in part to the fact that denial goes along with addiction. Addicts go to great extremes to hide their abuse from others—as well as from themselves. Once again, honesty is required to break the pattern.

As I mentioned in chapter two, even after I had faced into my own addiction to alcohol and stopped drinking, I still retained many of the behaviors of an addict. I finally had to realize that I was a dry drunk—no longer abusing alcohol but still in bondage to its many effects.

Drug Addiction

Drug addiction is oftentimes thought to be an issue for individuals who are morally weak. Many people don't have an understanding of how drugs affect the brain; it's much more than merely a social problem or a question of will-power.

When you are full of unresolved anger and turn to drugs to alleviate the pain you live with, you open the door to addiction and are at risk for negative changes in the brain that have serious long-term consequences. Repeated drug use affects a person's ability to make rational decisions and reduces self-control.

Someone might be able to use alcohol without becoming an alcoholic, but for those who are habitually angry, no mood-altering drug is safe. Take marijuana, for instance. It's a commonly held belief that smoking marijuana makes you mellow. But in truth marijuana only adds to a person's anger. Many angry individuals are also paranoid, and marijuana fuels this tendency toward suspicion and distrust.

Cocaine is notorious for creating hostility in those who use it. Many cocaine addicts struggle with this. PCP (angel dust), amphetamines (speed), hallucinogens (LSD), and opium (heroin) are all known to make people more aggressive, not less.

No matter what a person chooses as his or her drug of choice, mood-altering substances will only enhance the negative feelings that create the moods that lead to a habitually angry identity.

Pharmaceutical Medications

Taking pharmaceutical medications that have not been prescribed for you by a doctor or using them in a way that your doctor hasn't recommended can be more dangerous than you might think. It can even be fatal.

Prescription drugs are the third most commonly abused category of drugs, behind alcohol and marijuana and ahead of cocaine, heroin, and methamphetamine, according to the NCADD (National Council on Alcoholism and Drug Dependence). Overall an estimated 48 million people have abused prescription drugs, representing nearly 20 percent of the U.S. population.[7]

The prescription drug medications that are most commonly abused include *pain relievers, tranquilizers and sedatives*, and *stimulants*.

Prescription pain relievers include the opioid class of drugs, such as Vicodin, morphine, and codeine. Opioids imitate the body's natural pain-relieving chemicals, working with receptors in the brain to block the perception of pain. Opioids can produce drowsiness, nausea, constipation, and slow breathing. Opioids also can induce euphoria by affecting the brain regions that mediate what we perceive as pleasure. They are highly addictive.

Tranquilizers and sedatives depress the central nervous system. Xanax, Valium, and Librium—which are often prescribed to treat anxiety, panic attacks, and sleep disorders—are all in this category of pharmaceuticals. These depressants produce a calming or sleepy effect on the central nervous system.

Stimulants—which include Ritalin, Adderall, and Dexedrine—increase alertness, attention, and energy and are often prescribed for attention-deficit/hyperactivity disorder, narcolepsy, and depression. Stimulants enhance the effects of norepinephrine and dopamine in the brain, increase blood pressure and heart rate, constrict blood vessels, and assist the respiratory system. Like pain relievers, they can also produce a sense of euphoria.

Physical dependence on prescription pharmaceuticals can result from using them on a long-term basis. The body gets used to the substance, and then, if an individual stops taking the drug abruptly, withdrawal symptoms occur. Additionally the body builds up a tolerance to the drug, so higher and higher doses are required to achieve the same effects.

Like all drugs, medical pharmaceuticals simply mask the symptoms. They don't "cure" anything. A person might start out taking the drug as prescribed for an injury or some other chronic condition. But as time goes on, the person continuously tries to dull the pain and may resort to taking higher and higher doses. Suddenly the individual cannot make it through the day without the drug and has a full-blown addiction.

If someone decides to quit taking the pharmaceutical medication altogether, he or she will experience withdrawal. Symptoms can include restlessness, muscle and bone pain, insomnia, diarrhea, vomiting, cold flashes, and involuntary leg movements. A very serious risk is respiratory depression: A person's breathing can slow down so much that the person stops breathing completely, resulting in death.

Compulsive Spending

Alcohol and drug abuse are not the only forms of addiction. One of the most common is compulsive spending. This is just another way to take the edge off the pain one lives with from being habitually angry. Compulsive spending can take many forms, but basically it's a pattern of chronic shopping. The Illinois Institute for Addiction Recovery defines it as an "impulse control disorder" and says it shares the same features as other substance abuse addictions, but without any physical drugs or alcohol involved.[8]

Especially today, when credit cards are readily available and materialism is rampant in our society, people are focused on acquiring more and more possessions, and they put off paying for them until much later. Online shopping and television infomercials make it easy for someone to shop at all times of the day or night. Some questions to ask yourself about your spending habits are:

- Do I shop when I feel upset or disappointed?
- Do I spend money on things I don't need?
- Do I ever lie about how much money I've spent?
- Do I obsess over money and spending?
- Do I buy things on credit I wouldn't be able to afford if I had to pay cash?

Compulsive spending can provide instant gratification, making you feel temporarily happy. Quickly enough that euphoria wears off, and in its place are feelings of remorse, guilt, and shame. This just starts a vicious cycle of more spending. It can also lead to depression and other forms of abuse such as eating disorders. The shopaholic becomes addicted to relieving anxiety and other negative feelings by spending money on material things, whether or not he or she can afford them. Excessive spending is bound to affect close interpersonal relationships, as the spender seeks to hide his or her habits and debts. Many times things come to a head only when the situation is severe and requires drastic changes to resolve.

Gambling Addiction

A person who has a gambling issue can be defined as someone who bets something of value when the outcome is uncertain.[9] A gambling addiction can take many forms— playing the lottery, off-track betting (horse racing and dog racing), visiting casinos, and playing slot machines and table games. Even playing the stock market in a risky way can be the sign of a gambling addiction.

Gamblers often gamble to pay off other debts, and if they lose, they feel a strong desire to gamble again, confident that this time they will win. Pathological gambling has a negative impact on a gambler's family and home life; if left unchecked it can destroy one's career, deplete one's bank account, and ruin one's reputation. It can lead to crime, such as embezzlement.

If you grew up in a home with parents who gambled, you are more likely to gamble yourself. Statistics show that teens who are exposed to gambling at a young age are very susceptible to the thrill that gambling brings, and this can lead to serious problems at home and at school. Gambling is often called a "hidden illness" because there are no physical symptoms as there are with alcohol abuse, but according to the Illinois Institute of Addiction Recovery, pathological gambling is an addiction very similar to chemical addiction.

Internet Addiction

Internet addiction occurs when someone spends an inordinate amount of time on the Internet. An Internet addict becomes addicted to social networking sites or virtual communities. Time that should be spent on productive activities instead is eaten up with endless hours of "research" or watching YouTube videos and reading blogs. Those suffering from an addiction to the Internet often substitute virtual friends for the face-to-face human relationships they lack the skills to develop.

Some individuals suffering from this type of addiction may create online personas, which enables them to become someone other than who they really are. They may play video games incessantly. Individuals with low self-esteem or those who are addicted to the approval of others are especially susceptible to this. And physical issues can also result—from back problems and headaches to carpal tunnel syndrome and insomnia.

Many forms of behavior can become addictions if they are engaged in compulsively. Take texting, for instance, or continually checking email on one's smartphone. It's becoming common to observe couples sitting together at a restaurant, who, instead of talking to each other, are engrossed in their tiny digital devices.

Addiction is a form of escape. Learning how to manage one's anger in a positive way is vital for overcoming an addiction. Once an addict decides to give up his or her addiction—which is often used to mask anger—the addiction might be gone, but the anger remains. If the individual fails to deal with the anger, the risk of relapsing is great. Coping with and letting go of anger must be part of any treatment program or recovery plan.

Food Addictions

I have had the privilege of assisting many people who have crossed the bridge to success, yet that success only seems to exacerbate their struggle and feed their anger. They get so overwhelmed worrying about maintaining their success, feeling guilty about what they might do, angry about what they didn't do, and wondering how they're going to control the control of their future success that they tend to relapse and return to stuffing their angry feelings. The number one situation that causes people to relapse is not sedatives, medication, or alcohol—it's *food*.

Food keeps you overwhelmed. Anger—and guilt and shame about that anger—are the most typical commonalities that lead you to stuff your feelings. When you are overwhelmed, you require something to suppress those feelings of overwhelm. Understanding cause and effect is the key to looking clearly at the situations in your life and the perception of why you do what you do.

Overeating is not the only way people use food as an escape from their feelings. Those who have unresolved anger often develop serious eating disorders. Behaviors such as restricting the amounts or kinds of food consumed, binging and purging, and being addicted to excessive exercise often develop in response to emotional pain. Eating disorders may provide temporary control over distressing emotions, but they only lead to more physical and psychological harm.

Addiction-Free

I hit rock bottom at the age of thirty-two. I was a total addict, so chronically anxious that I wanted to take my life. I worried constantly about sleep—I couldn't go to sleep without alcohol, but by that point I knew that alcohol had to go. I would spend most of the day trying to talk myself out of drinking, hour after hour. It was exhausting. And eventually I would give in and have that first drink.

How did I ever let go of such an addiction? It wasn't easy, but it was worth the price. The day I went to my first AA meeting was extremely liberating. My first day of sobriety was such an emotional release for me—the tears just flowed freely down my face.

When I got clean and sober, one of the first things I had to ask myself was, "What am I going to do to put this inner fire out? What can I do with all this juice, all this energy?" I seduced myself into working out. I exercised two and three hours a day, every day, for about the first thirteen years of my sobriety. I used to run three miles a day. I used to play racquetball an hour or two a day. I lifted weights. I used to say, "I can't turn the engine off. I can't sleep at night—I might miss something," and I'd stay up all night. I did everything I possibly could to rid myself of the excess energy that burned within me. I didn't realize until much later in my career that what I was feeling was unresolved anger.

I went to therapists, I went to chiropractors, I went to Reiki masters—but I finally learned to let go in a place called hypnotherapy. I learned how to hypnotize myself, and I learned about the brainwave states called alpha and delta. I learned how to let go.

I've enjoyed twenty-five years of sobriety now through the grace of God, and I can honestly say I've never had a bad day, only a few challenging moments here and there.

If you punish yourself with alcohol, food, drugs, pharmaceutical medications, compulsive spending, and other forms of addictions to justify your low self-esteem, you are living in the anger, guilt, blame, shame, and resentment game. Events that are repressed, held onto, and unresolved are the reason you do what you do. Change requires addressing your feelings about yourself, letting go, and forgiving yourself and others one day at a time for the rest of your life. This new behavior is not hard—it's liberating and exhilarating.

If addiction has become your identity, one of the greatest challenges you will ever face is being honest with yourself and admitting that you're an addict. Letting go of an addiction requires courage and the ability to let go of the control that keep you controlling your addiction. Letting go requires a simple decision that the pain is great enough and you are no longer willing to live overwhelmed, in denial, and in an addicted state that holds you hostage. As you begin to do this one day at a time, you'll experience a gift you absolutely deserve: peace.

Ask Yourself

1. *Has anger led to a struggle with addiction in my life?*

2. *Has there been an addict in my circle of influence? If so, how has this affected me?*

3. *Am I willing to seek professional assistance for my addictions?*

CHAPTER FIVE
THE ANGRY GIVER

Anger is an uncomfortable emotion—being angry flies in the face of what we typically think of as acceptable behavior. However, anger is a universal emotion, and no one on the planet is exempt from it. Anger will always manifest itself in some way, no matter how hard we might try to ignore it, neutralize it, mask it, or hide it.

In our society women often have a more difficult time acknowledging their anger than men do. Traditionally many women were raised to believe that "nice girls" do not get angry. They may have been taught that anger was sinful or ugly. When these beliefs are internalized, anger doesn't disappear— instead it is hidden. Over time, it is even hidden from the individual; it's no longer recognized. If someone were to ask such a person if she is angry, she would deny it; she is no longer aware of it.

In the work world, good employees often habitually live in guilt. They know how to march to the tune of someone else. They are compliant. They'll go on being underpaid, overwhelmed, and then feel resentful because they're not getting compensated for what they're worth. Giving has become their identity. Think about it—and be candid and honest—in what ways have you been conditioned to give?

Giving is unequivocally a positive thing. There are many times when giving is spiritual. Giving can also bring you a great sense of satisfaction. "Jesus himself said: 'It is more blessed to give than to receive.'"[10] This is a statement you've probably heard many, many times. However, if you really break that statement down, you should be a good receiver, too—equally as good at receiving as you are at giving. Giving is noble, but so is receiving. In our culture there's a lot of guilt about being wealthy.

Angry givers are so focused on taking care of everyone else that they neglect themselves, which results in negative consequences in key areas such as health and finances. They put others' success and prosperity above their own, leaving them with plenty of guilt but very little money. Issues with intimacy often surface in their personal life because they're so busy taking care of others. In a marriage relationship, such an individual might attract a spouse who doesn't receive well, leading him or her to feel resentful and unappreciated.

Five Characteristics of Angry Givers

Angry givers say yes to everything. This is the type of person who can't or won't say no to anything. We could call them "yes-aholics." They are addicted to giving and serving. These individuals spend much of their time doing things for others—often things they don't really enjoy doing for people they don't really like. And while being altruistic and selfless is admirable (think Mother

Teresa of Calcutta), angry givers are actually motivated by fear and insecurity. They are seeking acceptance and approval, and they are afraid that others will reject them if they don't comply with every request. They are overly concerned about what people think of them. They over-give to the point that quite often they alienate the very individuals they attempt to serve.

Another word that describes the angry giver is *martyr*. Martyrs allow others to take advantage of their generosity and service and then suffer silently, hoping that someday their selflessness will be reciprocated. Oftentimes people who become martyrs were themselves taken advantage of as children. They may have been abused, violated, controlled, punished, threatened with abandonment, or made to feel shame or guilt, all which have led to a build-up of anger and resentment.

Angry givers appear to be in control. They like to rescue others; they gravitate to individuals who require "fixing." They are attracted to people who are broken, full of problems, and incapable of having normal, healthy relationships. Selfless givers are always ready and willing to take on other people's baggage and make it their own. They are the responsible ones in a relationship, allowing their partners to be irresponsible without any consequences. While angry givers appear to be in control, they actually live in a constant state of anxiety that the world they attempt so valiantly to hold together might someday explode and come crashing down around them.

This need for control typically stems from a fear of being controlled. Oftentimes these angry givers were raised by overbearing adults who demanded obedience from them, and as adults they have decided on some level never to be in that position again. Their sense of violation creates the effect of dominating others by taking such good care of everyone that those being cared for end up feeling smothered and controlled.

Angry givers are resentful. In spite of all they do for others, these individuals never feel recognized and rewarded fairly. They feel resentful because no one recognizes them for their contributions. They give to the point of exhaustion, and then end up sulking and full of self-pity. The result is drama and conflict because of how slighted they feel. They often wear a smile—an angry smile. People in their circle of influence know they can count on them because they are so dependable. "Can you run an errand for me?" "Could you possibly take me to the airport?" "Is there any way you can loan me some money?" (This really means: "It would really be awesome if I could seduce you into giving me money that I will never repay so you can feel disappointed and eventually resentful.")

Angry givers are unbalanced. Angry givers don't take care of themselves. Their entire identity is taking care of the kids, the parents, the grandkids, the neighbors, the co-workers, the boss. They are the servers of the world. If they are not taking care of someone else, they have no identity.

By over-giving, overcommitting, and overdoing, other areas of angry givers' lives fall apart. They refuse to delegate tasks to others out of a sense of perfectionism.

As their workload continues to pile up, they begin to miss deadlines and appointments. They overbook, overschedule, are continuously late, fall behind, and forget important information. Angry givers become so overwhelmed by their many obligations that they end up neglecting other important areas of their life. It is common for an angry giver's life to go from highly productive to a complete meltdown.

Angry givers can't allow themselves to relax. Relaxing is out of the question for these individuals because they have so much to do. They are too busy to relax...to slow down...to take a vacation.... They neglect the key areas of life that will bring them joy, happiness, peace, relaxation, and—most important of all—love. They are so busy they don't have time to enjoy their success; they are always focused on the next goal or accomplishment. These individuals never seem to have enough because *they* aren't enough.

From Angry Giver to Healthy Giver

If you're the type of person that has a bleeding heart, it's not always a negative situation. It just means you feel deeply about others. You are strongly empathetic, and not only do you feel others' pain, but you have a tendency to take on that pain. In the extreme, however, there are actually people that go out seeking to rescue others because it fulfills their biochemical craving, their addicted state of codependence. If this describes you, there's a high probability that your adrenal system is going to wear out. Your immune system, your lymphatic system, becomes compromised when you're in an overwhelmed state. You're consumed with caretaking, worrying, and over-obligating. This means that you say yes to everything, but then eventually you feel resentful of how many situations you've taken on. As Dr. Lynne Namka, author of *The Doormat Syndrome*, says:

> *Behind the intense caring for another person can be a hidden need for power and control gone awry. This is the same power drive that underlies all addictions. You give up your own personal power when you pursue any addiction of choice, be it alcohol, drugs, sex, a person, activity, or relationship. In codependency, the power drive manifests itself as the need to control the behavior of another person. It takes the form of rescuing, worrying, or obsessing over the other person. Mental energy is used to try to control the other person, thus ignoring personal responsibility for one's own problems. "I get to feel good because I take care of others" is distorted thinking.*[11]

If you recognize yourself in the description of an angry giver, be encouraged that there are ways to overcome and release this identity. You absolutely can learn to let go of your tendency to over-give. You can learn to value your time, and you do this by letting go of the belief that you are required to take care of everyone else.

You can learn to recognize the difference between priorities and demands. A priority is an event that is personally important to you; it's something that only you can accomplish. A demand, on the other hand, is a situation that is important to someone else but requires your time and effort to accomplish.

When you take on a project, how long does it take you to complete it? Do you over-analyze every detail? Do you fall into habits of perfectionism? Are you able to find a balance between focusing on the tasks at hand and taking time for recharging your own batteries? Or are you consumed with guilt and anger, unable to relax and enjoy the moment?

Learn to relax; life is not all about work or attending to the needs of others. Create new opportunities for yourself.

I've Been There...

Let me be really honest here. In my own life, there have been times when I have been so overcommitted to my success that I was just as guilty of over-giving as any of the individuals I've coached in my career. I had to learn from personal experience how to give myself permission to spend less time taking care of everyone else and more time relaxing.

I used to feel guilty taking vacations. I used to put off having a life. To develop balance, I'll let you in on a little-known secret: I love to read fiction. Fiction allows me to escape. For example, over a two-year period, I read every Louis L'Amour western written, and these were some of the most enjoyable moments I have ever spent.

Initially, if I was on an airplane with my employees, I

would feel too guilty to let them see me reading fiction. Finally, on one flight I just came clean and said, "Hey, fellas, look at this. This is called *Last of the Breed*. It was one of Louis L'Amour's last books. And this one's called *The Haunted Mesa*; it's one of the greatest spiritual books ever written. It's an awesome book, even though it's fiction." I love all kinds of fiction: crime fiction, war fiction, and historical fiction. I also enjoy the History Channel, DVDs, movies, experiences, and travel—but there was a time I had to give myself permission to do so.

I have a collection of classic cars. For years I just let them sit in the garage, but now I've learned to be able to take one of my classic cars out late at night, put the windows down, and feel the beautiful California air. What good is having a classic car that you never drive? It's time we all learn to smell the roses.

Too Angry to Receive

When you have unresolved anger, you might have an identity as a giver but are unable (or unwilling) to receive. For those who struggle with unresolved anger, receiving is often more difficult than giving. There are many reasons for this.

First of all, receiving creates a situation of connection. But those who are habitually angry shy away from too much intimacy. Their anger pushes people away and keeps them distant. Anger and hurt from past events creates a situation of defense. If you allow someone to get too close, you might get hurt again.

Angry givers feel a sense of control when they give to

others. But when someone gives to an angry giver, that control slips away, leaving him or her vulnerable. Giving is seen as a form of control, whereas receiving is seen as giving that control to someone else.

If you struggle with chronic anger, you may be uncomfortable receiving if your experience of this came with strings attached when you were growing up. Maybe you only received praise when you brought home a good report card or got a sports award. That type of receiving doesn't always feel safe—it might communicate that you aren't recognized for who you are but only for what you accomplish. Or you might sense that your mother was only interested in showing you off as a reflection of herself. That sense of being used made you angry, and now you don't trust anyone to sincerely give to you.

Angry individuals are prone to being suspicious of other people's motives. If someone does something nice for an angry giver, the typical reaction is "What do they want from me?" instead of gratitude for being given a gift. The angry giver sees others through hostile eyes, mistrusting their motives.

Learning to Give and Receive

Most of us have grown up with the idea that it's better to give than to receive. Unfortunately many times there is a disconnect between giving and receiving. Why do we develop the belief that it isn't great to do both? If we think of generosity only in terms of giving and putting others' needs before our own, this will greatly limit our ability to receive. But true openness of heart includes both giving and receiving. Focusing too much on giving can actually have the effect of closing yourself off from others.

If you are an angry giver, you may not be comfortable allowing others to assist and support you. But such a one-way street isn't healthy. It's your responsibility to grow and be responsible for yourself. Part of being responsible for your self-care is learning to receive from others. When you are nourished physically, emotionally, and spiritually, you are better able to nourish others, and you'll do so from a strong foundation of both giving *and* receiving.

You might have a perception that the people around you are unwilling to give to you, and in some instances this may be a fact. However, you can always seek out others who are willing to give. For example, why not treat yourself to a professional massage? Going out for dinner and being served as opposed to always being the one doing the serving is another way to receive. In other words, self-care doesn't mean just doing something for yourself; self-care also involves allowing others to do something for you.

Refusing to receive can lead to feelings of emptiness, resentment, and anger, just as giving for the wrong reasons can lead to those same feelings. But if you allow yourself to be the recipient of the gifts of others, you'll experience the joy of being supported, cared for, and loved. Learning to receive as well as give opens up the flow of abundance in your life. If you struggle with this area, this series of affirmations will assist you:

Now that I'm an adult…
- I'm becoming comfortable with both giving and receiving.
- I develop balance in my giving and receiving.
- I am comfortable with becoming a great receiver.
- I feel better about asking for what I deserve.
- I am capable of being honest about what I have accomplished.

Harnessing Your Anger

As you learn to let go of your anger, you can channel that energy; you really *can* harness it. You can use that energy to create a year you'll never forget. It will be your breakthrough year. But in order to do that, instead of being angry you have to learn to live in your peace. Your peace is your power. Your anger, while it feels powerful, is actually a huge energy drain. You might be able to turn it on for a few minutes or a few seconds, but it's exhausting. When you learn to live in your peace, you'll discover a power that energizes you to produce all day. You can produce full out all day, and when you go to bed you won't be exhausted.

If, however, you spend your day in anger and disappointment, you are usually wrung out before you go to bed. When you live in that kind of energy, you wake up exhausted. There is a high probability you will experience a body out of alignment. When you experience health issues, you'll be in denial about it, telling yourself, "I'm just under a lot of pressure."

What you're really under is the pressure of unresolved

anger issues. If you're late, overwhelmed, and you've got a lot going on in life, if you can't say no, if you're a people pleaser and you go out of your way to please the whole planet, it's very common to be angry and resentful because the people you're trying to please don't acknowledge you and your efforts.

Many times this starts in childhood. If you were expected to be a grownup when you were still a child, and now as an adult you're still taking care of everyone, there's a high probability you have unresolved anger. You aren't meant to take care of everyone. You *can't* take care of everyone. You must let go of being a people pleaser. You have to be able to please yourself. You have to be able to put yourself first occasionally.

If you're an angry giver who gives, gives, gives and never receives the recognition you feel you deserve, it may be because you're not producing results for yourself. You may be in management mode, attempting take care of everyone else's needs. Do you have to be in control of every situation? If you're so neurotically perfect that nothing is ever perfect enough, don't expect to have any peace.

I'm overcoming this myself. I've learned that this is a process. It's letting go of perfection so you can become effective. Being effective leads to success, while being neurotically perfect ensures you'll never get off the launching pad. It keeps you in a cycle of getting ready to get ready, which really means living in denial.

Ask Yourself

If being an angry giver has become your identity, it's time to take a good look at why you do what you do. Take some time to answer the following questions in your journal. If you have a hard time answering them, spend time thinking of ways you can rectify this situation. Be specific and dream big.

- *When was my last vacation?*
- *How often do I take time off just for myself?*
- *How can I pamper myself?*
- *When was the last time I did something just for fun?*

Before reading the next chapter, pick up the phone and call someone you haven't talked to in a long time. Send someone an email. Write a real letter. Reach out to someone on Facebook or Twitter. Most importantly, enjoy spending time with yourself. Live in the present and really let go. Let God.

CHAPTER SIX
PASSIVE-AGGRESSIVE ANGER

Unresolved anger from past events often results in individuals becoming passive-aggressive. This can be difficult to recognize at first, but eventually you can observe a disconnect between what a person says and what he or she actually does. There is a lot of hostility in passive-aggressive types, but initially you might not sense it.

What creates the passive-aggressive personality? Typically this occurs when a person is angry but believes that it is unacceptable to express that anger. The anger doesn't disappear, however; instead of being expressed overtly, it seeps out in covert, subtle ways.

Signe Whitson, LSW, author of *The Angry Smile: The Psychology of Passive Aggressive Behavior in Families, Schools, and Workplaces*, tells a story that illustrates this type of personality:

> *"Cash, check or charge?" I asked, after folding the items the woman wished to purchase. As she fumbled for her wallet, I noticed a remote control for a television set in her purse. "So, do you always carry your TV remote?" I asked. "No," she replied, "but my husband refused to go shopping with me*

and I figured this was the most evil thing I could do to him legally." [12]

This woman was attempting to avoid conflict in the short-term, but behavior such as this can lead to much more devastating long-term consequences.

Passive-aggressive individuals don't have the courage or integrity to speak openly and directly. Oftentimes this is the result of past events: being betrayed, ridiculed, treated as less than human, and hurt at a deep level.

If this has been your experience, instinctively you typically learned to hide yourself. You decided that to express yourself with an open heart would only lead to being hurt, demeaned, or abandoned. Most passive-aggressive people tend to have deep wounds, either from their childhood or from experiencing something traumatic at some point in their life. Fear and anger are a natural result.

Then, when faced with situations or people that trigger past events, an angry response arises, almost automatically and without conscious thought, stemming deep from within the subconscious mind. Next, emotions (anger, fear, bitterness) rise to the surface, but because they are perceived as unacceptable, the person represses the aggression and replaces it with a passive response.

However, instead of keeping the peace or maintaining the status quo, passive-aggressive tendencies drive others away. Without a solid foundation for connection and communication, without a sense of security and trust, there is no chance for a real relationship.

Here are some of the characteristics that angry passive-aggressive personalities exhibit:

Passive-aggressive individuals have identities of conflict and defiance. They might seem compliant and easygoing, but inside they are rebelling. They might not refuse to do things outright, but in the end they don't do them at all. When confronted, the passive-aggressive individual might pretend that he or she never heard the request or didn't understand what was being asked.

Passive-aggressive personalities have a sense of entitlement. They might be very talented, but they don't think they should have to work at anything—whether it's sports, schoolwork, or anything else that requires mastery. These individuals don't think they have to pay the price. They don't want to go through the process; they just want the payoff. They feel entitled to things, and then become even angrier when those things don't materialize.

Passive-aggressive personalities are full of hidden resentment. They do too much for people, setting them up to the point that they could never fulfill their expectations. This then allows the passive-aggressive person to justify his or her anger and resentment.

Passive-aggressive personalities are addicted to disappointment. They are masters of the blame game; they see others as the reason for their anger and disappointment. They hide behind a self-protective attitude, and this repels others, only reinforcing the disappointment they have come to expect and fueling their deep-seated anger.

Passive-aggressive personalities typically tend to be very pessimistic. They often perceive themselves as misunderstood; they can have a victim mentality. They have a warped view of the world in many situations, stemming from events from their past, and this leads to chronic anger issues.

I am a classic example of someone who used to have a passive-aggressive personality; I was addicted to resentment. I've been able to turn my life around, which is why I can assist other passive-aggressive personalities to do the same.

From Passive-Aggressive to Proactive-Assertive

Passive-aggressive individuals seeking to release unresolved anger often think that being assertive will be perceived as being aggressive. Not wanting to appear aggressive, they might slip into the opposite extreme—being passive. This just opens the door to more anger and resentment, so it's not the answer.

Assertiveness is a much different state than passivity, aggression, or passive-aggression. When you assert yourself, you clearly and calmly express yourself. You stand tall and make eye contact with others. You know what you require and aren't afraid to ask for it, but you don't do this at the expense of others.

In a *Huffington Post* article, British cognitive therapist Dan Roberts talks about a technique for becoming more assertive with challenging people in your life. He calls it the "Broken Record."[13]

State clearly what you would (or would not) like to happen, using "I statements" and being as specific as possible. For example, "I find it rude and frustrating when you interrupt me all the time, so in future please let me speak without interrupting. Thanks."

Let the other person respond—and try to let go of any expectations. They may accept what you say or they may not, that is their right. But it's also your right to stick to your guns, so then calmly and clearly repeat your point, as many times as you have to— do vary the words, so you don't sound like a robot! "Clearly you have a different view, which is fine. But the fact remains that it does really bother me when you keep interrupting, so please don't do it."

Repeat, as many times as you need to—in most cases, the other person runs out of steam and agrees.

Seducers, Sabotagers, and Loose Cannons

Passive-aggressive individuals are some of the most seductive people you will ever encounter. They can come across as very persuasive and easygoing. But they also are very unpredictable. They can suddenly implode, just like a loose cannon. These are the kind of people who absolutely go off the edge. And then, after an angry outburst, they promise it will never happen again.

Chronic passive-aggressive individuals typically move frequently; they are continually on the run from their past events. Often they live in denial, not even remembering the situation they created in the past because they are so smooth and so seductive—even to themselves.

I've coached many passive-aggressive individuals. They often are very successful, but they are also big sabotagers. They can literally sabotage an entire organization.

Many athletes fall into this category. Terrell Owens is a classic example of this. He was a talented NFL wide receiver who played for fifteen seasons. He holds (or shares) several NFL records and was a Pro Bowl selection six times. He caught 1,000 career passes, one of only nine players ever to do so. But there was another side to him. Wikipedia says: "As productive as he has been, Owens has been equally controversial, creating firestorms with almost every team he has played for as a professional."[14]

Back when Owens was playing for Philadelphia and at the top of his career, he loved to hold press conferences. He loved being in front of the camera. But after multiple episodes, he finally was relegated to the lowest rung of professional football, the Indoor Football League, with his hopes for another chance in the NFL long gone. And finally even the Wranglers released him. His actions both on and off the field led to many fines as well as penalties for the teams he played with.

There are many passive-aggressive anger addicts in sports today. Like Terrell Owens, they typically play for many teams, but teams typically eventually get tired of their behavior. They become known as malcontents, they're angry all the time, they blame other people, and they don't take responsibility for their own actions. They threaten to sue someone. They fire their agent. They are extremely unpredictable.

Eight Signs of Passive-Aggressive People

Here are eight ways you can recognize the passive-aggressive identity.[15]

1. Resenting the demands of others. When others make requests or demands of them, passive-aggressive people will often view them as unfair or unjust. Rather than express their feelings, they will bottle them up and resent the other person for making the demands.

2. Deliberate procrastination. Procrastination, the act of putting off that which needs to be done, is often a subconscious decision. With passive-aggressive people, however, it is often a conscious decision. Rather than tell the other person they cannot agree to the request, the passive aggressive person will delay completing the request until the very last moment, or later. This is a way of punishing the other person for having the audacity to make the request in the first place.

3. Intentional mistakes. Again, rather than saying no, passive aggressive people often find it easier to deliberately perform poorly at a task. They secretly hope they will not be asked again due to their substandard work.

4. Hostile attitude. As they often assume that others know how they feel, passive aggressive people tend to immediately assume that anything they do not approve of was an intended to be a jibe at them. For example, they may assume that their boss knows they have a full workload. When the boss makes a request of them, they assume he has something against them and wants to put excessive pressure on them.

5. Complaints of injustice. Passive-aggressive people see everything as a personal attack. When something doesn't go their way, it is seen as unfair or an injustice. It's all about how the world impacts them.

6. Disguising criticism with compliments. At first passive-aggressive people may seem pleasant and warm. They often appear to be complimentary. But many times their "compliments" actually are poorly disguised jabs.

7. The last word. Passive aggressive people love to have the last word. Even when an argument is over, they can't resist inserting one last insulting remark into the conversation. This remark is often more subtle than the ones which went before, but it allows them to feel victorious.

8. The silent treatment. Silence generally signifies agreement, but not the way passive-aggressive people use it. It effectively communicates their displeasure or rancor, but it does so in a way that negates the possibility of collaboratively resolving the situation.

Let Go and Live

Awareness is the first step. Releasing passive-aggressive tendencies that stem from unresolved anger requires facing your fear, anger, and past wounds; it requires learning to express yourself authentically.

Owning your feelings, words, and actions takes

courage, but moving into a state of emotional liberty is grounding and freeing. It takes time and space to release the effects from toxic past events, but the alternative is to remain locked in a cycle of pain and misery.

If you are ready to let go of passive-aggressive behavior and begin living a life you enjoy, here are four ways to get started.

Learn to ask for what you want. Let go of the assumption that those around you should know what you want without you being required to articulate it. Drop the pleading, whining, and cajoling, and state your needs clearly and calmly.

Don't confuse wants with requirements. A requirement is essential for survival—think food, water, air. Wants, on the other hand, make our lives better, but we are absolutely able to survive without them: new cars, bigger homes, expensive vacations. Don't fall into the trap of exploding over something that isn't all that important. Know the difference between a want and a requirement.

Know the difference between priorities and demands. Priorities are events and situations that are personally important to you—only you can accomplish them. Priorities are personal. Demands, on the other hand, are events and situations that are important to someone else but require your time.

People-pleasers and angry givers typically become accustomed to fulfilling the demands of others at the expense of their own priorities, which only leads to resentment and anger. Be clear about what is truly important to you, and then when someone else demands your time or attention, calmly assess whether you are able or willing to fulfill it.

Instead of being an angry producer, become a relaxed producer. Let go of the frenetic energy that stems from anger. That energy might actually produce results for you, but at what price? Instead become a relaxed producer. Learn to pace yourself. You'll find that you accomplish more than you ever did when you allowed anger to drive you.

Being relaxed is a synchronistic space where you are able to create with ease. Skill, persistence, habits, and a winning mindset all combine to allow you to live from a relaxed intensity. This results in a quiet, cool, silent power. It enhances your vibration to a state where synchronicity begins to occur effortlessly.

During this year, plan at least a three-day vacation. Take mini breaks. Instead of being consumed with work, work, work, focus on results and the time required to achieve those results. Develop the ability to produce more with less effort, and then spend that valuable time with your loved ones, the people who deserve to feel your warmth and your spirit. Learn to put the same energy you put into serving, giving, and producing into relaxing, because you unequivocally deserve to receive it all.

Your Anger-Free Zone

The more you understand the cause that creates the effect, the more you'll realize that events shape feelings. Feelings become moods, and moods become an identity. As you begin to live one day at a time, the better you'll become with this process. When people start saying to you, "You have really changed," you will know that you're making progress.

Signs of Your New Identity

- You no longer fly off the handle.
- You don't automatically feel violated.
- You don't have to get on the phone and prove yourself right.
- You don't have to get in the ring with someone.
- You don't have to be controversial.
- You don't feel compelled to fire off emails or Facebook messages.
- You can stop and take deep breaths.
- You avoid conflict as much as possible.
- You stay out of drama and chaos.
- You learn to neutralize other people's emotional states when they are not conducive to peace.

Ask Yourself

1. *Has there been someone in your past who was passive-aggressive? What kind of a relationship did you have with this individual?*

2. *In what situations do you exhibit passive-aggressive tendencies? Describe what typically triggers this behavior in you.*

3. *Think of an area where you have had difficulty asking for what you require. How could you reverse this situation and express yourself honestly?*

CHAPTER SEVEN
HOW ANGER SABOTAGES YOU

There is a strong correlation between fear and anger. A person with habitual anger typically has a lot of underlying fear. This can manifest in many ways:

- Fear of rejection
- Fear of money
- Fear of success
- Fear of intimacy
- Fear of commitment
- Fear of responsibility

Being angry is one way to mask these fears from others, and even from yourself. It can be a way to protect yourself from feeling weak, ashamed, embarrassed, or vulnerable. But it unfortunately leads to struggle, which absolutely does not lead to success. It takes a lot of emotional energy to stay in the struggle. It takes a huge amount of emotional energy to stay broke. And yet angry individuals continue to insist on struggling. When they are just about to turn a corner and reach the success they have been dreaming of, something happens that sabotages them.

Cause and Effect

Understanding the cause behind the effect is required to change this destructive pattern. The key to preventing self-sabotage is understanding *why* you do what you do. That's the only way you'll be able to make new choices. It's all about cause and effect.

When I stopped drinking, I was addressing the effect. That was a huge step, but eventually I had to address the cause. In my case, the cause stemmed from events in my childhood. I didn't realize this until I was an adult, but it led to a lot of issues in my life. Even though I was intelligent and talented, I would consistently sabotage myself. My life was a series of "up the down staircases." Up, up, up; down, down, down—I was always coming in through the out door.

I've been called "the millionaire coach"; many of my students have gone on to be successful, and a few of them have achieved the status of millionaire. But one of my greatest skills is assisting my clients to address the physical and emotional addictions that keep them from breaking through. I assist people to go back to the beginning—to understand the cause behind the effect. If you don't understand the cause, then you will live in the effect.

During my early career in free enterprise, I would typically find a company and work my way to the top of the compensation plan—and then the company would go out of business. This wasn't just a one-time event; it was a pattern. A company going out of business was the effect, but eventually I had to dig deeper and address the cause. I had to address the reason I chose such companies.

After I got sober, I spent the next fifteen years getting comfortable with myself, learning how to love myself, becoming my own best friend. This involved letting go of many patterns. It required letting go of anger.

I created the term "Hostile Young Man Syndrome" to describe myself. I grew up with a lot of unresolved anger based on past events that happened during my childhood. I was picked on as a child, and my response to this was anger. I experienced some violations. My parents were both teachers, and my dad was also an athletic coach, and because of this I was teased and bullied. It was very uncomfortable having my parents at school with me.

I didn't really know how angry I was; I kept my feelings deep within. However, I took my anger out by using drugs and alcohol. Throughout my twenties, I stayed very angry in my addictive state; I had a lot of hostilities. I would tend to get into fistfights—I was constantly in trouble. I went from being an all-American boy to hitting rock bottom due to the pull of the addiction rabbit hole.

Situations always seemed to happen to *me*. I would attract situations where I would get arrested, get into trouble, get involved in one conflict or another. Conflict became a way of life for me. I had a conflict consciousness. I would get "in the ring" frequently, always ready to fight. People would do things that were preposterous to me. I would go to great lengths to attract people and situations that would fulfill my anger.

I grew up with a lot of hostility, and while I certainly directed it toward those in my path, much of it was directed inwardly toward myself. This Hostile Young Man Syndrome went on for years.

The Sabotage Cycle

Remember when you were a child, full of dreams and aspirations? You were free back then; you were naturally spontaneous. Where is that little child? What happened to those dreams? Keep asking yourself why, and eventually you'll get to the heart of the matter. Who stole those dreams from you? Who replaced them with anger, disappointment, and fear? Who conditioned you not to be successful?

If you're like most of us, by the time you were eighteen years old, you most likely heard the word *no* 144,000 times. What kind of philosophy of success did your parents have? Did they encourage you to live life on your own terms? Or did you watch them struggle? All of this early conditioning formed your own beliefs. Struggle, fear, worry, anger, failure—this is the cycle of sabotage.

Those who live with unresolved anger are very familiar with this sabotage syndrome. If key people in your circle of influence were inconsistent, angry, abusive, or full of worry, there's a high probability that today you regularly experience anxiety about the future. This creates an overwhelmed state, and anger is often the result. Full of angry emotions you try to ignore, you develop a pattern of avoidance. You are afraid of failing so you are resistant to trying new things, and there's a loop that plays over and over in your mind: "I don't want to fail." You avoid situations you perceive as having the potential for failure.

But what you don't understand is that you fail in a much more significant way. By failing to engage, you are missing out on life, and that's the biggest failure of all.

You are waiting for the perfect, mythical, magical moment, but it never happens. The tooth fairy doesn't show up. The success genie never appears. All that happens is that you continue to live in that overwhelmed, disappointed, so-called "safe" space. But what is the result? You feel a new wave of anger and guilt because you are not acting on the opportunities that present themselves. Your anger turns into resentment as you see other people succeeding, seemingly overnight.

In my coaching practice I've assisted hundreds of professionals to build and sustain tremendous success over time, and I've assisted many of them to release the anger issues that were destroying the success they so desperately were seeking, shattering their dreams and goals. Whether it is success in a career, financial success, or successful relationships, too often people aren't aware of the part they play in destroying their chances for success and happiness. They are oblivious to how they repel the very outcomes they desire.

Angry Perfectionists

Anger often manifests itself as perfectionism. There is nothing that leads to sabotaging success more than requiring yourself to be perfect. Nothing and no one is good enough for an angry perfectionist. From personal relationships to workplace woes, perfectionism is a virus that leaves a wake of destruction. Perfectionism is a way to stay in control, and it opens the door to all kinds of angry reactions.

I struggled with perfectionism for years, and I've experienced the damage it caused in my relationships. No one could ever live up to my standards. I expected a level of cleanliness in my home that was unattainable and unrealistic. Dirt, hair, all kinds of little things would drive me nuts. Every room had to be perfect. I vacuumed compulsively—in precise rows. I actually kept a vacuum in every room in my house. This enabled me to have a measure of control.

All of this control led to anger when things weren't "just so," and as a result I was never emotionally available to those closest to me.

Let's examine some of the characteristics of the angry perfectionist.

Angry perfectionists are hypercritical. They are extremely judgmental and see everything as all or nothing, black or white. There is no middle ground. They are especially critical of themselves, however. This is why they shy away from opportunities that involve trial and error. They can't afford to make mistakes.

Angry perfectionists seek to be flawless. Such individuals are usually very well-appearing. They dress neatly and are extremely meticulous. Their appearance masks a deep-seated anxiety, and they often suffer from depression. All this stems from their unresolved anger issues.

Angry perfectionists are loners. They feel most comfortable when they work alone. They push themselves to work hard, often to the exclusion of any kind of balance in their life. Work is a way for them to channel their anger, and they prefer not to collaborate with others. They are so focused on their own perfection that they literally have no time for others. Long ago they learned that relationships can be painful, and the anger they carry from past events hinders them from being open to those around them.

Angry perfectionists have to be in control. Being in control assists angry individuals to feel less vulnerable. And while they might prevent that sense of vulnerability, they can't possibly control everything to the degree they desire, which leads to disappointment and more anger. It's a vicious cycle.

Angry perfectionists typically wait a long time to marry. They are so sure that others will disappoint them that when they do find someone to marry, they end up sabotaging the relationship because of their controlling ways.

Angry perfectionists have conflict in the workplace. They can obsess about any number of things and experience continual issues with co-workers and bosses. Their angry perfectionism negates any real success they could have, because there is no success without collaboration with other people. They end up alienating the very individuals who could be their strongest allies because they insist on being right. They have angry outbursts and provoke arguments.

Angry perfectionists don't understand the difference between perfection and excellence. They are more like machines than human beings. Somewhere along the line perfectionists shut off their emotions and just tried harder to live up to the expectations of some authority figure—a parent, a teacher, an older sibling. They developed the belief that if something wasn't perfect, it wasn't enough. This is a very destructive pattern; sooner or later the individual begins to think, "I am not enough." This only leads to more anger, more striving, more perfectionism. Angry perfectionists have a high degree of anger turned inward on themselves.

Once perfectionists are able to release their anger, they can begin to take some risks. They begin to realize that the people around them aren't looking for machines or robots—they want to see humanness, not some artificial perfect state. People actually are inspired by someone who is transparent enough to cry—not tears of self-pity or anger, but real tears of joy or compassion.

Angry Produceaholics

A variation on the angry perfectionist is the angry produceaholic. This is an individual who uses anger to focus on producing results. Producing results sounds like a positive situation, but when anger is the root, it's a different animal. Production has become the produceaholic's identity. What typically happens is that these individuals become so driven by their anger that other areas of their life suffer. Intimacy, hobbies, friends, and spouses all fall by the wayside in the pursuit of production.

I used to be an angry produceaholic. But today I've learned to be a peaceful relaxer instead. I enjoy taking vacations. I've learned to take mini-breaks. I was forty years old when I first heard the words *relaxed intensity*, and those two words changed my life. Up until that point, all I knew was "intensity." I can now produce in a relaxed intensity, and my business has never been more successful.

Money Issues

Financial issues create many opportunities for anger and self-sabotage. Getting money right is very important. If you are uncomfortable in any way with money—how you feel about it, what you do or don't do with it, the way it impacts your daily life—it's vital that you begin to examine your relationship with money.

Our beliefs about money typically start in early childhood. I grew up with two educated, hardworking parents, both who had master's degrees in education. Our family was thrifty and economical, and we lived a non-consumptive lifestyle, although we always had nice things. I was raised with good values and a solid work ethic. My parents taught me that income was earned the traditional way, but as a young adult, I knew that wasn't the path I wanted to take. I dreamed of being financially independent and achieving big dreams. I've shared some of my struggles along the way, but eventually, part of dealing with my anger involved getting right with money and moving into a prosperity consciousness.

If you're like most people, you've eaten 20,000 meals with the wrong financial planners by the time you were eighteen. Perceptions about money are typically passed down generationally from great-great-grandparents to grandparents to parents to children. You can think of this as a "money message." It's usually a message of scarcity. When you were growing up, you may have been told:

"We can't afford it."

"Money doesn't grow on trees."

"You'll just be disappointed if you buy that."

"Rich people can't be trusted."

"Money is evil."

These types of statements shaped your perceptions around money, causing you to feel disappointment, guilt, anxiety, and anger. You might be ashamed that you have so little money; this might make you feel angry when you look around at others who seem to have so much more than you do. When shame and anger are involved, no amount of money is ever the right amount.

Many individuals feel anger and fear when it comes to handling money. I've worked with many clients who were despondent when they had to pay their bills or pay down credit card debt. They were reluctant to part with the money they had because doing so left them feeling deprived. Issues from the past regarding money can be the cause of a poverty consciousness that colors how we see the world—the opposite of an abundance mentality that views the world as a friendly, safe, generous place.

Most of us are used to viewing money as something independent from us; we are not accustomed to thinking that our use of money is a reflection of who we are. This takes a high degree of honesty—it requires getting real with money and our relationship to it. It requires letting go of the fear and resentment, the guilt and shame, the anger and remorse we've accumulated around the issue of our finances. This can be difficult because typically we've all made some pretty poor choices where money is concerned. However, the results can be far greater than any difficulty we have in taking responsibility and choosing to change our relationship with money. Money doesn't have to be your enemy—it can absolutely be your friend!

The Attractor Factor

If you continue to live the same situation over and over, you will continue to experience the same results. For instance, if you continue to attract people who make you feel guilty, or who make you feel uncomfortable, it's a sign that you are operating from a place of low self-esteem. When you live in shame from events from your past, you continuously send a very mixed, very low vibrational signal. The result is that you will attract the same situation over and over. People in such situations are subconsciously attempting to fulfill old feelings of guilt and shame, but this only leads to resentment.

Maybe you grew up in a family with a tyrannical mother or grandmother. Or maybe you had an overly aggressive father or grandfather. Maybe there was alcoholism in your family, which typically leads to passive-aggressive tendencies. As a child, perhaps you learned that you had to walk on eggshells. You learned to be careful about what you said. You never wanted to upset someone. You felt you had to explain, validate, and justify your existence.

There's a high probability you learned to tiptoe quietly through life, not wanting to upset anyone. I coach many clients in this situation who are seeking to be successful entrepreneurs. Now as adults, they feel guilty about making a phone call to solicit business. They are concerned about coming across as too pushy. Asking for a commitment makes them feel guilty, so they never really get clear about what they have to offer or what they require to close the sale or secure the project. Instead they stay trapped in an overwhelmed state of worry and fear.

You don't have to stay in the sabotage syndrome. As you let go of your anger—as you face into the cause that creates the effect in your life—you will experience a new openness to life. You'll be free to try new things, develop close relationships, and strive for excellence (not perfection). Instead of anger, fear, and anxiety, you'll live in joy, confidence, and peace.

Ask Yourself

1. *What forms has anger taken in my life, and how has this sabotaged me?*

2. *How has perfectionism contributed to the anger in my life? How has it kept me from realizing the dreams I had as a child?*

3. *As a way to begin making peace with money issues, I will look back through my life and honestly assess the top three mistakes I've made with money. I will allow myself to feel any anger that might surface as I face into this. I will consciously let go of these old memories, these old mistakes, and in their place, I will create a space in my consciousness for new abundance and prosperity.*

CHAPTER EIGHT
ANGER AND YOUR HEALTH

Anger is a very interesting energy. In some situations anger actually can lead to producing results. For example, sports figures (who are typically in excellent physical shape) often use anger to fuel controversy and public acclaim. These individuals seem to thrive on the energy and fanfare that anger produces, but they can become so controversial that they become alienated from the general populace and create enemies, hate, and outrage.

But what their anger doesn't create is peace. Our bodies don't function well when we operate in chaos, drama, anxiety, or overwhelm. What these situations create is a neurological state where serotonin levels drop and stress levels increase. Serotonin is a chemical found in our bodies that is thought to contribute to well-being and happiness; it also assists with mood balance.

There's no getting around it: A large percentage of society is in an overwhelmed state, full of anxiety and anger. Most of the population is dealing with abandonment and rejection issues, and for many in our society, their drug of choice is food.

The Mind-Body Connection

Our bodies and minds are always connected, and a general principle is that the body obeys the mind. In other words, the body will manifest the beliefs of the mind. Belief is a powerful thing—what we believe exerts tremendous power over us, and we see the effects in our bodies. The more negative we are, the more we will tend to accept negative thoughts and ideas, whereas a positive person is able to reject the same ideas as untrue or unacceptable. Our thoughts are very powerful; they operate at an extremely high vibration. As David Hawkins says in *Letting Go*, "A thought is actually a thing; it has an energy pattern. The more energy we give it; the more power it has to manifest itself physically."[16] He goes on to say that this is the paradox of much so-called health education:

> *The paradoxical effect is that fearful thoughts are reinforced and given so much power that epidemics are actually created by the media (e.g., the swine flu). The fear-based "warnings" about health dangers actually set up the mental environment in which the very thing that is feared will occur.*[17]

Individuals that are holding onto a lot of anger, fear, or resentment are all candidates for physical illness and disease. If such individuals can learn to let go of these negative effects by changing their thoughts and beliefs, positive health will result.

Alcoholics Anonymous has long taught that no lasting recovery is possible unless an individual undergoes a fundamental change in personality and consciousness. The founder of AA totally changed his beliefs and underwent a complete transformation. Marty M., the first woman in Alcoholics Anonymous, experienced this, too. Her doctor confirmed that she went from being an angry, intolerant, selfish individual full of self-pity to someone who was forgiving and full of love.[13]

Louise Hay is well-known for connecting how prolonged emotions, feelings, and moods create dis-ease (disease) in the body. In her book, *You Can Heal Your Body*, Louise references several ailments, conditions, and diseases that can manifest from anger.[19]

In my recovery process from drugs and alcohol, I developed a migraine headache that lasted for seven years. My neck frequently would subluxate, or move out of alignment, causing pain and discomfort. I became obsessed with going to the chiropractor daily, and sometimes I would go to multiple practitioners in one day. I also had a tendency to grind my teeth, which developed into TMJ (temporomandibular joint) disorder. I would take my anger with me to bed at night and wake up with a headache. Although I had committed to being and staying sober, I was now left with the effects of the past events that I had not resolved. My body was holding onto anger, and I no longer had the alcohol and drugs to numb what I was feeling.

As I continued to search for a solution to the challenges I was experiencing, I began to uncover the connection to my emotional state. The TMJ was rooted in anger, resentment, and a desire for revenge. My neck challenges were related to stubbornness and inflexibility, and they were rooted in the mistakes I hadn't forgiven myself for. I was stuck in the past, refusing to let go of my self-judgment. The neck is also the narrowest place in the body, and much of my energy was restricted in this area. My mind would not allow an outlet for my frustrations, and so there was a blockage of energy in and around my head. Self-criticism, pressure, and unresolved anger resulted in my migraine headaches.

By developing an awareness of the root cause of the emotions, feelings, and moods that had become my personality, I now had the opportunity to create change and move into a more peaceful existence. I was able to begin addressing these past situations that were part of my neurology. I began to uncover the cause-and-effect relationships that led to my addictions, low self-esteem, anger, and the dis-ease in my body. I made a conscious decision to begin letting go and release what no longer served me. In that letting go process, I was able to release the TMJ, the migraine headaches, and the subluxations that had plagued me in my early sobriety.

The following are some of the conditions that can manifest from anger: lockjaw, TMJ, neck problems, pimples, blackheads, warts, styes, urinary tract infections, bad breath, Bell's Palsy, boils, bursitis, carpal tunnel syndrome, cold sores, wounds, and lower back pain. Many people who suffer from sacral pain are "sitting on old anger." Stubbornly holding onto past events related to unresolved anger is the cause of their pain.

Negative Disease-Producing Beliefs

The effects of unresolved anger create negative beliefs, and those negative beliefs can lead to disease. Here are some questions to ask yourself to determine whether your beliefs might have a negative effect on your health:[20]

- Am I guilt-ridden?
- Do I hold a lot of anger inside?
- Do I condemn other people's behavior?
- Am I judgmental?
- Do I hold resentments and grudges?
- Do I feel trapped and hopeless?

The way to change your health is to change your thoughts and feelings. When you let go of negative thoughts and beliefs, you also shed the negative emotions that give them energy.

Habitual anger can wreak havoc on a person's immune system. Problems with digestion, skin problems such as eczema, rosacea, and acne, food issues such as anorexia and bulimia, fatigue, and a host of other aches and pains can all result from anger's toxicity.

Anger has a direct correlation to your health. The effect of anger has been known to further the cause of cancer, multiple sclerosis, and many other maladies. Anger can also cause your adrenal system to burn out. It can have a negative effect on your lymphatic system. Anger can blow out your neck. A constant release of stress hormones can cause harm to many of the systems in the body, resulting in long-term health challenges if anger is not addressed.

Waking Up Angry

If you wake up angry, there is a high probability that your neck or back is out of alignment because of how much pressure you are putting on yourself. Unresolved anger creates TMJ, which means you grind your teeth at night. If you are shaking your head right now, thinking, *Yep, I grind my teeth,* realize that you do not grind your teeth because you are a "tooth grinder." You grind your teeth because of unresolved issues you continue to hold onto.

Anger in and of itself doesn't create pressure. Anger creates an emotional state that consists of a very frenetic energy. This can create subluxation in the neck—specifically C1 and C2—and it can also affect the lower back on the non-dominant side of your body, often causing one leg to be longer than the other. Anger usually shows up in the non-dominant side of your neck. You also grind your teeth at night on the non-dominant side of your body. If you're right-handed, it's very common that you'll grind your teeth on the left side of your jaw.

I've been there, as I've mentioned. My dentist even gave me an occlusal splint, a mouth guard designed to protect the teeth from the adverse effects of TMJ. I sawed right through it. I used to go to the chiropractor every single day—and I do mean every single day, seven days a week. I was so controlling and so smooth in my unresolved anger that I had a series of chiropractors I seduced into seeing me off the clock, even on Sundays. I am not proud of this, but I share it to show you I had my own issues with control.

It became so chronic that I could predict when my neck was going to go out because of how angry I was. In those days I actually got addicted to the crack that happened when I had my neck adjusted. That crack, however, did not mean that my neck was actually going back into place. It just meant that the neck was releasing nitrogen, and nitrogen is very similar to an opiate, very similar to dopamine, which provides the feel-good factor. I became addicted to that release.

My father was a very fiery athletic coach, and as I mentioned, both he and my mother taught at the same school I attended. He was also very opinionated. Other kids picked on me because they did not like my father. I felt victimized by being bullied, so I took boxing lessons. I turned my boxing lessons into overt anger. I also took out my anger and aggression by playing sports. At the time I thought it was a good outlet for a feisty, fiery young man, but this wasn't the case.

The Cortisol Connection

Cortisol is a hormone found in the adrenal glands; it is essential to the maintenance of equilibrium, or homeostasis. Often called "the stress hormone," cortisol regulates the changes that occur in our bodies in response to stress. Some of the areas cortisol influences include blood sugar levels, immune responses, blood pressure, heart and blood vessels, and the central nervous system.

Chronic stress tends to elevate the levels of cortisol in the body. This causes negative effects, such as:

- Compromised cognitive performance
- Lower thyroid function
- Blood sugar imbalances
- Decreased bone density
- Sleep issues
- Damage to the immune system
- Increased belly fat
- High blood pressure
- Loss of muscle

In particular, increased abdominal fat is more detrimental to your health than fat stored in other places in the body. This increased belly fat has been linked to heart attacks, strokes, higher levels of LDL (the "bad" cholesterol), and lower levels of HDL (the "good" cholesterol).

Unresolved anger, whether it's overt or covert, causes a high level of stress, producing high levels of cortisol, which is very detrimental to health. Elevated cortisol levels have been shown to interfere with learning and memory, to lower immune function and bone density, and to increase weight gain, blood pressure, cholesterol, and heart disease. Chronic stress and elevated cortisol levels also increase the risk for depression, mental illness, and lower life expectancy. Cortisol is released in response to fear or stress by the adrenal glands as part of the fight-or-flight mechanism. This type of energy, fueled by anger, is not conducive to optimum health.[21]

Anger can also lead to exhaustion, and this creates low levels of cortisol, which can lead to adrenal fatigue. Negative effects of too little cortisol include:

- Brain fog
- Depression
- Low thyroid function
- Fatigue—especially morning and mid-afternoon fatigue
- Low blood pressure
- Inflammation

Anger and all its associated feelings (guilt, shame, resentment) can lead to your body producing too much or too little cortisol. It creates a situation of being stuck in fight-or-flight mode, worried about a future outcome that has not yet happened. You tiptoe around; you use terms like "walking on eggshells" and "being on pins and needles." You are stressed out and exhausted.

Releasing unresolved anger is required to restore a healthy balance. Learning to manage stress, getting adequate sleep, and eating a healthy diet are practical, positive steps you can take.

Anger Hurts Your Heart

Recent studies have shown a link between anger and heart disease.[22] People who frequently experience high levels of explosive anger are at risk for elevated blood pressure, a quickened heart rate, and atherosclerosis (a build-up of fatty plaque in the arteries), or stroke. Anger seems to affect men's hearts more negatively than women's.

For example, one large study published in *Circulation* in 2000 found that among 12,986 middle-aged African-

American and white men and women, those who rated high in traits such as anger—but had normal blood pressure—were more prone to coronary artery disease (CAD) or heart attack. In fact, the angriest people faced roughly twice the risk of CAD and almost three times the risk of heart attack compared to subjects with the lowest levels of anger.[23] According to a study conducted by the University of Sydney, "the risk of a heart attack is 8.5 times higher in the two hours following an angry outburst."[24]

Anger may not be the only factor in heart disease risk, but angry individuals are typically full of other chronic negative emotions such as anxiety and depression, which have also been linked to heart attacks.

But just as you often can lower your cholesterol and blood pressure by diet and exercise, thus decreasing your risk for heart disease, lowering your anger level also can have a positive effect on your physical health. The next time you feel yourself getting ready to fly into a rage, stop and think: *Is it really worth risking a heart attack?*

Anger and Your Liver

According to Chinese medicine, most organs are connected to an emotion.[25] Your liver is the main organ connected to anger. The liver's main purpose is detoxification. It filters the chemicals that enter the body, but if your liver is unable to perform this action, toxins will be stored in order to keep them out of your blood. In today's society, the typical diet and lifestyle contributes to the liver storing a multitude of toxins.

In Chinese medicine, it is believed that a toxic liver

ANGER AND YOUR HEALTH

leads to anger problems and with people having issues controlling or letting go of their anger. Over time, toxic habits worsen the situation. The following habits can exacerbate this condition: smoking, taking drugs, and regularly eating junk or processed foods, or GMOs.

When your liver is toxic, you'll feel anger longer, more intensely, and more passionately, and you'll have a difficult time letting it go. It can become an overwhelming, overpowering emotion that gets the best of you and affects the people in your circle of influence. Accumulated toxicity in the body and the liver from unhealthy diets and lifestyle choices play an important role in the effect on your emotions and behavior.

According to Louise Hay, the liver is the seat of anger and primitive emotions. Liver challenges can arise from chronic complaining, justifying, faultfinding, deceiving yourself, and feeling bad. Author Sabrina Reber says:

> *On an emotional level, if you frequently experience irritation, impatience, being overly critical, rage, hate, angry outbursts, over-reactivity, feelings of not feeling heard, not feeling loved, not being recognized, judgment, racism, the need to control, inability to express your feelings in a grounded and balanced way, lack of joy, denial and inability to be honest with yourself and others, inability to be authentic, or any addiction of any kind, you may want to consider doing a liver cleanse. Cleansing the liver can rapidly accelerate your spiritual growth because you expel*

the calcified stone of anger you create in your liver whenever we can't process through your anger.

Your body protects you when you are angry and not able to release the anger, so it takes the energy of anger and creates a stone. These stones build up in the liver and block the flow of life force energy within your being. A lack of life force energy means a lower vibration, less light, and an unhealthy body. Releasing stones, stored emotions, and feelings help you to activate more of your DNA strands, enhance your light, create more Joy for yourself and have a more balanced and grounded Life. In addition, when you activate the four additional codons within your being the body will NOT be able to store anger anymore. Stored anger from the past in the form of stones must be released or your liver and gallbladder will act up, prompting you to cleanse so you can raise your vibration to the appropriate frequency, thus reaching your highest soul's potential.[26]

Eating Disorders

Eating disorders are serious emotional and physical problems. The most common eating disorders are anorexia, bulimia, and binge eating disorder. Recent studies have shown that higher anger levels have been reported in those that have eating disorders.[27] In particular, those that are bulimic had a higher rate of suppressed anger.

With any eating disorder, suppressed emotions tend to be the underlying cause. Engaging in an eating disorder allows you to avoid and suppress your feelings. According to Thomas Wadden, MD, director of the Center for Weight and Eating Disorders at the University of Pennsylvania's medical school, people who swallow their anger feel, for whatever reason, that they can't express it, so they resort to food.[28] Courtney Pool, a health coach who specializes in healing compulsive eating, has personally experienced the effects of anger regarding food issues. She shares her story:

> I realized that underneath my food compulsions was anger I had from my childhood and how I was treated, anger at how people throughout my life had hurt me, anger at how I felt like life was overall just too hard in so many ways. I had rage at how fed up I was of having a food addiction, how much it had limited my life, how much I hated it, how hard I was trying and how impossible it seemed to change. I was angry that I had a food addiction and weight issues, and I was angry that I had to heal my food addiction at all. I was even angry that I was angry! Sometimes, the anger I felt was even more like hysterical rage. But I didn't want to think of myself as someone who had "anger issues" or rage. It conflicted with my self-image.[29]

According to the National Eating Disorder Association, eating disorders can create a range of health challenges and complications. The following are the most common types and adverse health effects:

Anorexia Nervosa

Anorexia nervosa occurs when there is an inadequate food intake leading to a weight that is clearly too low. Because the body is denied the essential nutrients it requires to function normally, it is forced to slow down all of its processes to conserve energy. This can lead to serious medical consequences. A person engaged in anorexia may have an abnormally slow heart rate and low blood pressure, which mean that the heart muscle is changing. The risk for heart failure rises as the heart rate and blood pressure levels sink lower and lower. Often there is a reduction of bone density, accompanied by muscle loss and weakness. Severe dehydration can occur, which can result in kidney failure. Fainting, fatigue, and overall weakness are common effects as well.

Bulimia Nervosa

Bulimia nervosa is characterized as consuming very large amounts of food followed by behaviors to prevent weight gain, such as self-induced vomiting. These binge-and-purge cycles can damage the entire digestive system. Purging behaviors can lead to electrolyte and chemical imbalances in the body that affect the heart and other major organ functions. Other health consequences include electrolyte imbalances, which can lead to an irregular heartbeat and possibly heart failure and death, inflammation with the possibility of rupturing the esophagus from frequent vomiting, and tooth decay from stomach acids released during frequent vomiting.

Binge Eating Disorder

According to the National Eating Disorders Organization (NEDA), binge eating is the most common eating disorder in the United States.[30] People with binge eating disorder have episodes of consuming very large amounts of food but without the behaviors to prevent weight gain, such as self-induced vomiting. The food is consumed rapidly, and the result is extreme discomfort, accompanied by feelings of shame and guilt. Some of the potential health consequences of binge eating disorder include: high blood pressure, high cholesterol levels, heart disease, type II diabetes, gallbladder disease, fatigue, joint pain, and sleep apnea.

Laxative Abuse

Laxative abuse can often accompany eating disorders, because it often seems like the perfect solution to ridding the body of extra calories. A person using laxatives to get rid of calories or as a weight loss tool can create a very dangerous situation for his or her health. Typically, someone abusing laxatives believes that the food won't be absorbed, thus reducing calorie intake, but this is far from the truth. The reality is that by the time laxatives take effect in the large intestine, most foods have already been absorbed into the small intestine, along with the corresponding calories. The perceived weight loss due to laxatives is really nothing more than water weight.

Laxative abuse can cause electrolyte and mineral

imbalances, severe dehydration, kidney damage, and internal organ damage may result, including stretched or "lazy" colon, colon infection, and Irritable Bowel Syndrome. Chronic laxative abuse may contribute to the risk of colon cancer.

Lose Your Anger and Improve Your Health

Buddha once said, "Holding onto anger is like grasping a hot coal with the intent of throwing it at someone else; you are the one who gets burned." Especially in the area of physical health, the effects of holding onto anger have devastating effects. But what happens if you learn to let go? What if you replace anger with peace? With forgiveness? Here are just some of the positive benefits you can expect when you make the choice to release your anger:

- Lower blood pressure
- Less back pain
- Better sleep patterns
- Healthy heart rates
- Higher levels of HDL, the good cholesterol
- Fewer headaches

A detox is another way to assist your body to release pent-up anger. There are many benefits to cleansing and detoxing the body. Over time toxins accumulate in your major organs and tissues. The detoxification process removes the toxins and excess waste the body has been storing. As you detoxify your body, organs like your liver will begin to function more effectively. Typically your immune system will be stronger and your blood will circulate better. You'll feel lighter and more energetic.

Doing this provides your body with the opportunity to function at its highest level. One of the greatest benefits, especially for releasing negative emotions like anger, is strengthening your state of mind. When you clear out the brain fog, you are in a better space to respond instead of react.

As you gain a better sense of well-being, you open the door to improve all areas of your life and reach your full potential. Here are a few modalities you may consider trying:

- Liver Cleanse
- Kidney Cleanse
- Master Cleanse
- Cellular Cleanse
- Raw Food Cleanse
- Juice Fasting
- Intermittent Fasting
- Colon Cleanse
- Epson Salt Detox Bath
- Skin Brushing
- Oil Pulling
- Infrared Sauna
- Steam Shower

I personally had a top-of-the-line steam room installed in my home for the purpose of detoxifying my mind and body. I typically steam two to three times a day, and it provides a haven for me to reflect, meditate, and release.

I highly recommend that you find modalities that allow you to bring your body and mind into balance. By giving your body a chance to rest and recharge, you are creating an optimal situation for releasing anger tendencies.

Ask Yourself

1. *Am I currently struggling with any health issues? Have I ever stopped to wonder if they could be due to the anger I am carrying?*

2. *How positive are my thoughts overall?*

3. *What is my reaction to negative suggestions and thoughts from others?*

PART THREE
RELEASING ANGER

One surprising observation about the mechanism of letting go is that major changes can take place very rapidly. Lifetime patterns can suddenly disappear, and long-standing inhibitions can be let go of in a matter of minutes, hours, or days. Rapid changes are accompanied by an increased aliveness. The life energy set free by the letting go of negativity now flows in positive attitudes, thoughts, and feelings, with a progressive increase of personal power. Thoughts are now more effective. More is accomplished with less effort. Intention is made powerful by the removal of doubts, fears, and inhibitions. With the removal of negativity, dynamic forces are unloosed, so that what were once impossible dreams now become actualized goals.

DAVID R. HAWKINS, *LETTING GO*

CHAPTER NINE
LETTING GO

In Part One, we looked at the roots of anger, and in Part Two we covered the effects of anger—emotionally and physically, on ourselves and on others, on relationships, on careers, and on everything in between. Now we're ready to get serious about letting go of anger.

I used to feel guilty because I believed I wasn't good enough. I couldn't seem to breakthrough to success. I exhausted myself getting exhausted. I overwhelmed myself with my brilliant ideas that someday, mythically, magically, would come to fruition, and I would rescue myself and my family. This was a story I repeatedly told myself. But guess what? My family didn't require being rescued. I didn't require being rescued. What was required was an understanding of cause and effect—an understanding of why I did what I did.

As I slowly learned to let go, this became a more common way of life. I had to learn that letting go is not physical; letting go is emotional.

You let go by first making a decision that you don't have to know how to let go. Letting go is not a how-to exercise. Letting go is a very simple equation: Letting go is *letting go*. The reality is that there is nothing to let go of, because you don't control anything physically. It's all about emotional control. What you're holding onto, clinging to so tightly—your guilt and shame and worry—is a myth. There's really nothing to worry about because nothing actually has happened.

Worrying is an exercise in futility. Worry keeps your brain occupied: You think you're so busy, but you're really being incredibly nonproductive, and this eventually leads to guilt. Now you feel bad about what you didn't do. You get overwhelmed; you have challenges resting, so you require some outside sedative or substance that allows you to stuff your feelings. The key to breaking this cycle of addiction is understanding your emotional state. The more you understand the cause that creates the effect, the less likely you are to go back into a state of denial.

When you learn how to let go of (or release) your anger, you let go of (or release) your feelings about events. When you're able to separate yourself from the facts, the facts remain the facts. Learn to let go of your feelings about an event; change your perception about a situation; change your language when you talk about these things. Let go of getting even. Have you ever sat around and plotted how you might get even with someone? It's a colossal waste of your time.

I'm not suggesting that you always turn the other cheek, but I am suggesting that you learn to let go. Let go of what you have no control of. Let go of what's not going to serve you. Let go of what's going to burn your most valuable commodity: time. Address what you have to address and move on. These days, for instance, when someone says unfavorable or ridiculous things on Facebook, it's much easier to simply delete the post, block the person, and move on. Rather than getting into a debate with someone, it's best to just let go of the situation. Learn to erase the event. Take a deep breath, and let go.

When you take a deep breath, it releases your neurological network. A deep breath is virtually a reset button that reprograms your perception of past events. For a few seconds and a few minutes, when you take that deep breath, it neutralizes the past and releases your anxiety about the future. When you're able to let go of anxiety about the future, it prevents you from going into a drunkalogue, a whole dissertation, or a diatribe about what might happen.

The Benefits of Letting Go

Letting go involves a huge release of inner pressure. If you've struggled with unresolved anger, you know what it feels like to have the weight of the world on your shoulders; letting go is feeling the burden of that weight drop away. You're left with a feeling of relief. You feel lighter, happier; you feel free.

Once you recognize the accumulation of anger along with all the other negative emotions that go along with it, you can make a decision to surrender and let go. This opens the door to positive feelings, a new spontaneity, and a peaceful calm.

Letting go is powerful. You can expect to experience

a real transformation as you release the blocks that have kept you from enjoying achievement and fulfillment in your life. In fact, many new areas of life can begin to open up for you. Instead of the constricted, small space you previously occupied, you'll begin to experience life as a wide-open expanse of opportunity and choices.

David Hawkins describes how differently life can look—and how full of love—when we let go:

> *One delightful discovery we will make is that our capacity for love is far beyond what we ever dreamed. The more we let go, the more loving we become…. As this happens, our life becomes transformed. We look different. People respond differently to us. We are relaxed, happy, and easy-going. People are attracted to us because they feel comfortable and happy around us. Waitresses and cab drivers suddenly mysteriously become attentive and courteous, and we will wonder, "What has come over this world?" The answer to that question is "You have!"*[31]

The goal of letting go is more than just getting rid of negative emotions and addictions. The ultimate goal is total freedom and total peace. And one side effect of letting go of anger is that it leads to letting go of many other negative feelings (anger's companions), so your whole life is transformed.

Although letting go might sound simplistic, its effects are truly profound. A small surrender can effect a major change in your life. Can it really be that easy? Your perceptions might be that all the anger and negativity that has been so much a part of your life for so long couldn't possibly be eliminated so simply. But once you understand how the mechanism of surrender works, you'll be surprised at how much ground you can cover in a short amount of time.

Before going on, take a few minutes to make a conscious decision to stop resisting and be open to surrendering, to letting go.

Neutralize Your Anger

Neutralizing anger is a key component in the recovery process. Begin to understand what triggers bring up feelings of anger for you. Develop a greater awareness of the people and situations that spark your emotions. Don't fall prey to anger invitations. Someone may be late to an appointment, cut you off in traffic, spill coffee on your shirt, or make a sarcastic comment. If you accept these invitations to be angry, you will enter a perpetual cycle of being stuck. By no means am I saying you should hide from your feelings of anger, but instead learn to find an awareness of the triggers and politely decline the invitation.

Say no to the bait of an argument. Decline to engage in conflict. Let go of feeling that you have to be right. Learn to disengage. Own your feelings and take responsibility for them. No one can make you angry. *You* get angry. Anger is a choice. Begin to neutralize situations where your anger is typically triggered. Anger is a part of life, and it can be an indicator of challenges or problems that arise, but if anger is a part of your daily experience, you are saying yes to too many invitations.

As part of the process of releasing anger, you must learn not to jump to conclusions; you must learn to let go of over-exaggerated perceptions of situations that arise. Instead become a problem solver. Speak calmly and talk slowly so you can express your feelings clearly. Most importantly, remember to breathe. With practice you can release the urge to yell, scream, curse, and explode. You can communicate with a calm and relaxed disposition while clearly communicating your point, your position, or your dissatisfaction.

If you have passive-aggressive tendencies, let go of irritating others and creating frustration for them. Begin to release tendencies that make your demeanor unpredictable. Let go of playing games with people for your amusement.

You may gain a sense of pride or power in proving you are right and showing others they are wrong, but when you do this, you will never attract the people to your life that will bring you joy and prosperity.

If you have tendencies to over-give, over-obligate, or save people, if you are a "yes-aholic," it is now time to let go. Letting go releases the angry-giver identity. Learn to empower people instead of rescuing them. Begin to let go of seeking acceptance from others, and begin to accept yourself. You no longer require engaging in codependent behavior. Begin to slow down, relax, and focus on the key areas of life that will bring you joy, happiness, peace, relaxation, and love.

Begin to focus on the people, situations, experiences, and successes you want in your life, and let go of focusing on what you don't want. Where you focus and put your attention is where you will live in your emotional state. Begin to breathe in the energy of peace, abundance, and flow.

The Simplicity of Letting Go

Once you face the fact that you have an issue with anger and are ready to let go of it, how do you actually do it? Letting go is not physical; it's not linear. There are very few books written on this topic. One of the best is *Letting Go* by the great David Hawkins, quoted above. However, letting go can be done right here, right now. Letting go is nothing more than a decision. It is not complicated. Letting go is simple. It is so simple that most people want to complicate it. They want a formula. They want a blueprint. They want guidance. They want coaching. They want mentoring. They want a pastor. They want an AA sponsor. They want someone to tell them how to let go.

How is the most overrated word in the dictionary. The most underrated word that will give you peace, spirit, emotion, and freedom is *why*. Your focus should be on why you do what you do. You should be aware of why you want to overcome the challenges facing you. This is your why. If you don't have whys—reasons to let go, reasons to succeed, reasons to dream—then you'll tiptoe quietly through life and experience the greatest regret of all, the pain of regret. You want your epitaph to read,

"Here lays a man (or a woman) who got all they ever wanted." (That's a great line from a song called "Living in a Moment" by Ty Herndon, a song that was number one on the charts in 1999.) If you continue to focus on your why, you will unequivocally get a great result.

Letting go begins with your words. Your words are your law, and your words do not return void. If you continue to say, "This always happens to me," you have created an expectation that you will fulfill through your biochemical feelings that will transmit and transmute ethericly. That means your law of attraction will attract people and situations to fulfill your low self-esteem.

To affirm means "to state." Affirmations have power. Affirming that you are letting go sounds like this:

"Now that I'm grown up, I no longer attract violators and perpetrators who emotionally abandon me and victimize me.

"Now that I'm grown up, I'm letting go of my feelings that no longer serve me."

"Now that I'm an adult, I am comfortable with who I am becoming."

Begin to state your affirmations with the words "now" and "I am." The words you choose to use have power. For example, when you use the word *need*, this is a future-tense word with no commitment.

"I need to change."

"I need to stop getting angry."

"I really need to get a new life."

Affirmations are extremely effective in assisting you to let go. Affirmations must be believed, however. An affirmation without a belief is merely a wish. It's merely empty words. When affirmations are words of belief—when you believe what you're saying and you can write and speak your affirmations in the present tense—they are incredibly powerful.

Because I've struggled with anger and learned to let go of it, I now can assist you to do the same. I no longer am obligated to hold onto my anger. I came to the place where I said, "On this day, I cast my burden on the Christ within. I no longer hold Joe Smith responsible for my feelings."

Writing a letter to someone can also be effective. Write a letter to yourself and then burn it, letting it go. You might burn some sage, which is a Native American custom that can rid the body—or a house—of negativity. Negativity breeds anger; anger breeds negativity. They go hand-in-hand.

When you continue to hold onto the ties that bind, you are virtually emotionally locked into a set of feelings that create an emotion. That emotion will continue to attract a similar situation over and over. You then say to yourself, "This always happens to me."

I have coached many business owners and entrepreneurs who are in the process of building teams and acquiring employees or salespeople. The fact of the matter is that a large percentage of the population is not going to be responsive to the opportunity being offered to them. They won't understand the risk-for-reward principle. Many of them will be underachievers—starters and not finishers. I coach my clients to let them go and not get angry, to meet people where they are. Many of my clients tell me they don't understand the people they come across. People are driving them nuts. My response is that people are predictable. Learn to meet people where they are. Don't set people up to fail you.

Anger in Our Culture

We live in a conflict-driven culture. Special interest groups are everywhere. It's common for people to relate to each other with high suspicion, vehemently expressed opinions, and even open hatred. In this type of environment, anger is often seen as a virtue.

Today the media is a big part of our lives. It's very interesting how anger shows up in social media and other forms of media. Around election time, you will see two or three parties start to accuse each other of certain situations. You can see anger and hostility in commercials when it comes to debates. Just recently various groups have rioted because of ethnically charged situations. In today's media age, it seems that, no matter what the topic, political issues can only be discussed in angry rants. The old-fashioned form of polite discussion about the issues of the day all too often deteriorates into a shouting match. The media is famous for stirring up situations because that's what sells. As part of releasing anger, I recommend refraining from watching the daily news.

Flaw Finders

Frequently you're going to encounter people who look for and find the flaws in anything. I call them "flaw finders." They will find the flaw in you. They'll find a flaw in life. They're addicted to finding flaws. If you've had flaw finders in your past, when you encounter this type of individual, your typical reaction will likely be anger. Learning to let go requires learning to spot this personality type—it means learning to operate intuitively. You must learn to intuitively feel, touch, and sense these kinds of people and not engage with them.

Learn to spot people who set you up to disappoint them. They brood and pout; they make negative comments. Before anything happens, they're negative. They make fun of people. They make derogatory comments about those in leadership. This type of person typically lives in a dark cloud. They are spiritual and emotional vampires. They are people you unequivocally want to avoid.

When Anger Is Justified

How do you know when anger is justified? This is a very interesting question because there are absolutely times when anger is justified. Most of us have been conditioned to *repress* our anger. But how about being conditioned to *release* our anger? Too often we stuff our anger.

Anger is justified, especially when it's released. When you've been violated, traumatized, abandoned, neglected, abused, beaten, or bullied, there's a high probability you'll be angry. Your anger is justified in these situations. Justifying it means recognizing it, understanding it, being aware of it, and not holding onto it. Holding onto anger will allow you to continue to stuff it with food, alcohol, or some other substance. When you're angry, feel your anger—but then release it quickly.

When you're angry, recognize it. When someone does something to you and you start to feel yourself go over the cliff or you have a wall-kicking moment, be candid about it. Be honest. Find someone that can walk you through it, talk you down from the ledge. Take some time to write in your journal about the experience, but most importantly, learn to forgive. When you forgive someone, that doesn't make them right. It doesn't make them wrong, either. It lets you out of the situation emotionally so you're not holding someone else responsible for your feelings.

Events that happened five years ago, ten years ago, twenty years ago, or thirty years ago occupy space in your emotional wall if you hold onto them. They stay in your subconscious. When you continue to hold onto a parent or other individual for something they did, you're the one who's the victim, and you're giving them power to be the victor.

The real question isn't whether your anger is justified. A more important question is whether your anger leads you to act in a way that honors your deepest self. Your anger might be justified, but the real issue is how you choose to express that anger. If you do so in a way that clearly states the issue, and does so in a calm, thoughtful manner (versus in an impulsive, reactive way), you'll have a much better chance of releasing the anger and not holding onto it.

The Land of Letting Go

Once you let go of anger and no longer feel the requirement to eat compulsively or be an exercise fanatic or a compulsive drinker, what can you replace those addictive behaviors with? Breathing, peace, reading, letting go, spending time in a relaxed type of exercise are some suggestions. Many times angry people take their anger into the gym. You can see them using punching bags or weight lifting. They make loud sounds. They want to be noticed.

Peace will allow you to let go of your unresolved anger. You want to be able to spend the second half, or the second two-thirds, or the last quarter of your life in the emotional state called peace, where your energy vibrates from love, joy, bliss, and enlightenment. You want to be able to operate from awareness rather than from anxiety, fear, and doubt.

What does daily life look like when a person releases unresolved anger from past events and learns to let go? Let's examine some characteristics of individuals who have learned the art of surrender.

The outer world no longer is the source of their happiness and fulfillment. Those who have learned to let go understand that true happiness comes from within. No longer must they look to outside sources for meaning.

They are compassionate, supportive, tolerant, and appreciative of others. They see the value of others and no longer feel the need to compete or judge them. Instead of striving to control others, they seek to assist them to grow and reach their potential. While they see themselves as serving others, there is no sense of giving out of a sense of duty or martyrdom. Their relationships are meaningful, and they have a strong connection to others.

They are vibrant and energetic. They are productive and "in the flow" of life. Free from addiction and defeat, they make wise lifestyle choices and reap the benefits of health and vitality.

Life is seen as full of opportunities—not challenges. They awake each day with a sense of anticipation and expectancy. Every day brings new situations to explore, new relationships to develop. No longer is life seen as one long struggle, with one problem after another.

As part of the letting go process, it's important to take your health into account. You may consider changing your diet in order to increase the amount of nutrition you provide your body. This does *not* mean going on a diet; it means staying away from fast-food choices and artificial sweeteners and choosing higher quality water. It means fueling and nourishing your body in a manner that allows you to operate at your best physically and emotionally.

Healing Modalities for Letting Go of Anger

As part of the letting go process, it's important to release anger that is stored in the body. Repressed anger becomes stored emotional energy. Over time it will build until you either reach a breaking point or you begin to experience physical symptoms and disease (dis-ease). The following practices can assist you to release negative emotions and begin to regain balance in your mind and body.

Breathing

Breathing is one of the easiest ways to allow your mind and body to function at their best. It is a great de-stressor and can result in calmness and relaxation. Breathing techniques can bring about a sense of awareness and mindfulness. When you engage in the practice of breathing, you oxygenate your brain, which can reduce anxiety levels. This will allow you the opportunity to gain clarity and insight to any challenges with anger that arise.

Dr. Andrew Weil, a well-known physician in the field of holistic health, says, "Practicing regular, mindful breathing can be calming and energizing and can even help with stress-related health problems ranging from panic attacks to digestive disorders."[32] On his website (www.drweil.com), you can find specific breathing exercises.

Exercise

Your physical and mental health has a strong connection. Exercise is an outlet for releasing stress and pent up energy. According to Nathaniel Thom, a stress physiologist, "exercise, even a single bout of it, can have a robust prophylactic effect"[33] against the buildup of anger.

When you engage in exercise, your heart rate increases, which pumps more oxygen to the brain. Recent research has shown that exercise increases growth factors in the brain, which makes it easier for new neuronal connections to form. Rewiring your neural network is a key component to releasing anger patterns.

Yoga

Yoga has many healing benefits on the mind and body. This practice, which is more than just a physical exercise, relaxes your sympathetic nervous system—your fight-or-flight response. It also regulates your adrenal glands, which secrete cortisol. Increased cortisol sparked by anger or other negative emotions can lead to increased food binges. Because yoga aids in regulating the adrenal glands, cortisol levels are more balanced. While practicing yoga, your blood pressure drops and tension in your body releases. This creates a space for you to quiet your mind and slow down your thoughts of anger, guilt, shame, and resentment. One of the greatest benefits to practicing yoga is that it assists you to build awareness and release your feelings of anger.

Meditation

Meditation can allow you access to your subconscious mind. Because the subconscious mind is where you hold past events and memories along with your beliefs, oftentimes you are unaware consciously of the many emotions that are attached to your beliefs and linger from the past. When you engage in meditation, you access the subconscious and are given the opportunity to explore emotions that may have been previously hidden. One of meditation's greatest benefits is emotional release. According to Yoga International:

> *Meditation is a precise technique for resting the mind and attaining a state of consciousness that is totally different from the normal waking state. Meditation is a practical means for calming yourself, for letting go of your biases and seeing what is, openly and clearly. It is a way of training the mind so that you are not distracted and caught up in its endless churning. Meditation teaches you to systematically explore your inner dimensions. It is a system of commitment, not commandment. You are committing to yourself, to your path, and to the goal of knowing yourself.*[34]

Hypnosis/Self-Hypnosis

Hypnosis is a modality that uses guided relaxation, intense concentration, and focused attention to achieve a heightened state of awareness. This can be done with a trained therapist or through self-hypnosis techniques. Hypnosis involves your subconscious mind, where it may provide access to buried memories and emotions that keep you in a state of anger. By focusing on the mental programming that causes you to feel so much anger, you have the opportunity to reprogram and release it.

Self-hypnosis audios are another option to address

the subconscious mind. By reprogramming your unconscious mind, hypnosis can assist you to remove bad habits and tendencies toward anger while replacing them with positive and proactive thinking.

Massage/Body Work

Massage can have a powerful effect on your body and emotional state. Because so much stress is held in the body, massage and body work release the tension that builds in the muscles and tissues. Massage has the ability to aid in anger management because it can decrease anxiety, release emotional muscle memories, rewrite old emotional patterns, create new neural pathways in the brain by releasing old muscle/emotional habits and patterns, enhance the quality of sleep, improve concentration, increase circulation, and reduce fatigue. Letting go of old feelings, habits, and memories are key components to releasing the past and stepping into peace.

Acupuncture

Acupuncture is a healing modality that originates from China. It involves the insertion of very thin needles through the skin at specific points on the body. According to the San Diego Center for Integrative Medicine,[35] acupuncture therapy can release blocked energy in the body and stimulate function, evoking the body's natural healing response through various physiological systems. Acupuncture strives to balance the organs related to your emotional state. As part of this process, it assists in the process of releasing anger by triggering relaxation, reducing stress, and creating a sense of well-being.

Other Healing Practices

Other healing practices to explore include Reiki, chiropractic care, craniosacral therapy, and EFT Tapping (Emotional Freedom Technique). You may want to consider a liver cleanse, a cellular cleanse, a colonic, a detox bath, or any other wellness-related practices that allow you to release the toxic build-up in your body. I myself have done many different types of cleanses and detox programs in order to restore my body after years of drug and alcohol addiction.

Just Let Go

Letting go is...letting go. It's a simple choice, a simple decision. People often want to make it more difficult than it is. Don't rent space to people who don't deserve it. Don't give your time to people who no longer require it. Don't waste your energy on situations you can do nothing about. Don't continue to hold onto what doesn't serve you. Move on, let go, release, and be in the present. Begin to use this affirmation:

> *I am me. I am free. I am no longer the sum total of the past events that created my overwhelmed state. I no longer give my power to being anxious.*

Most importantly, stop worrying. What value does worry bring you? Absolutely nothing. Then don't give it energy.

Don't focus on what hasn't happened, and don't worry about failing. So many people create a situation; they invent a story about the future. They avoid the perceived situation that never happens, and then they become angry at themselves for this.

Let go of any story that does not serve you. Stop being angry with yourself. Begin to love yourself. Start to change your identity. Be a lot more objective. Tell yourself, "I'm not failing—I'm just starting." Stop using words like *hard*. Don't say, "Oh, this is so hard!" You'll only perpetuate your struggle and then be angry for not succeeding. Let go of your anger. When you start to let go of your anger, people will notice. They'll say things like, "Wow, you look really different. You look really good."

Holding onto anger ages you. It shows up in your eyes. It shows up in the creases on your forehead. It shows up in your abdomen. A lot of times people will carry an excess of five to ten pounds of unresolved "angry" water weight.

Another great exercise is yelling. Yelling gives you a deep primal experience into the rage and violations that you've held onto for so long. Take a towel, fold it over a couple of times, bite down on it, and scream as long and as loud as you possibly can. If you do that two or three times in a row, you'll be amazed at what happens in your body. It's almost an out-of-body experience. When you really get into the spirit of letting go and give voice to some of that repressed rage, you might feel lightheaded for a few minutes. But you'll also feel like you just released five or ten pounds. Your shoulders and neck will loosen up from releasing the excess unresolved emotional anger you've been holding onto.

When you begin to let go of your anger, what do you replace it with? Love. When you replace anger with love, you begin by loving yourself. You discover a different love for the universe. You have a new love for animals, a love for people, a love for Scripture, a love for self-improvement, a love of love. When you come from that kind of energy, you begin to really understand who you are in the world.

You can be the person you know you're capable of becoming. At last you can stop judging yourself, belittling yourself, stuffing yourself, damaging yourself. You look in the mirror—and whether you're 120 pounds or 240 pounds—you know inside of you there's a person of greatness. You might find yourself in tears, but these are tears of compassion and gratitude. It's very different from all the tears you once cried when you were a victim.

When you can cry from the depths of your spirit, these are tears of relief. You now are transmuting and transmitting an entirely different energy. When you come from that place, you can speak objectively about what you've been through. You can be honest, objective, and real. You can freely admit that you're an addict, or that you've been violated, or that you've done things you're ashamed of. This level of authenticity allows you to heal, and it all starts from admitting what you've struggled with. Otherwise you'll just stay in the same place. You'll stay overwhelmed, angry, judgmental, and resentful about the person you're not meant to be. You'll remain stuck being the person you don't want to be because you don't have the courage to be the person you could be. Being the person you could be would contradict the person you've become, and it requires tenacity to face this head on. You don't change because success would contradict your struggle.

Letting go means letting go of your own identity. It means reinventing yourself. As you begin to let go of the old you, the old victim, the old average person, the old identity, the old self that no longer serves you, you are in the process of recovery. You are in the process of prosperity and reciprocity—you are reinventing yourself. You are becoming a whole new energetic being. Vibrationally you will begin to transmit and transmute a whole different set of feelings as you let go of the events that are no longer your identity.

You let go of events by making a decision. You let go by making a commitment. The more you are able to filter an event, the more you let go of an event, the better chance you have to regain your power. When you are uptight, when you get ready to get ready, when you are in fight-or-flight, you over-analyze and over-process, and this is what you have to let go of. You have to let go of your analytical, egoic mind that requires being perfect. You have to let go of having to know all the answers, always feeling that you have to know what to do and who to be, always being overwhelmed. When you move into that space, you begin to change your energy. When you move into that "let go" space, you will unequivocally begin to change what you attract!

The Thirty-Day Anger Detox

Because letting go is a process, it's beneficial to have some concrete steps you can implement in your life. What does an anger detox consist of? It's taking deep breaths throughout the course of a day. It's not eating the foods that you would typically turn to and crave when you are angry. It's not giving power to people who don't require it or deserve it. It's learning how to meditate. It's letting go quickly. It's smiling more frequently. It's waking up with a different type of mindset. It's changing your emotional energy. It's having dedicated blocks of time to do what you're committed to doing. It's following through on your word, one day at a time. It's starting something—and finishing it.

The following Thirty-Day Anger Detox can assist you to release your anger in practical and tangible ways.

1. Practice taking deep breaths during the day.
2. Make a conscious decision to eat nutriously.
3. Learn how to meditate; start with five to ten minutes every morning for the next month.
4. When anger rises up in you, let go quickly.
5. Pray the Serenity Prayer each day.
6. Give yourself permission to yell into a folded towel as long and as loudly as you want.
7. Take a walk.
8. Plan your next vacation.

9. Smile frequently and notice the effect on your mood.
10. Plan your workday; make blocks of time to do what is required.
11. Clean and organize your living space.
12. Follow through on your word.
13. Take a break from TV (the electronic income reducer).
14. Forgive someone you've been holding a grudge against.
15. Write a letter to someone you've lost touch with.
16. Express gratitude to a family member.
17. Read a personal development book for thirty minutes each day.
18. Only check your email once in the morning and again in the evening.
19. Call a friend to offer some encouragement.
20. Create a set of affirmations and read them each night before falling asleep.
21. Look your best; develop good grooming habits.
22. Tackle something you've been procrastinating about.
23. Journal about past hurts or violations and then write a paragraph letting them go.
24. Take responsibility for the way you feel about a particular situation.
25. Replace every negative thought with a positive one during the course of your day.
26. Don't give your power to someone who doesn't deserve it.

27. Stay calm for an entire day.
28. Hire a coach.
29. Choose to let go of negative feelings instead of expressing them.
30. Instead of berating yourself when mistakes occur, gently affirm yourself and move on.

CHAPTER TEN
RELEASING ADDICTION

How do you break an addiction that does not serve you? There are several components to this equation. You break an addiction by being aware of what you are about to do that does not serve you. You take a deep breath and release the feelings connected to the event. Surround yourself with people who are in recovery and learn to address your feelings one day at a time.

You do not have to hit rock bottom to let go of your addictions and experience your biggest breakthroughs. This is a chapter that is not required in your life story. The best time to change or address any addiction is now. Only you can decide when the pain is great enough. When you reach the point that you no longer require the pain to be your identity, you will let go and begin your process of recovery.

Breaking any addiction comes down to a definitive moment in time when you—and only you—can answer this question: "Is the pain great enough?" When the answer is unequivocally yes, you will let go and begin to live one day at a time.

An anger addict will always require a little bit more of the chemicals released in the brain to get the emotional high. According to Dr. Joe Dispenza, featured in the movie *What the Bleep Do We Know!?*, "If you can't control your emotional state, you must be addicted to it." When you are angry all the time, your personality is creating your personal reality.

Releasing an addiction requires rewiring your neural network. Nerve cells that don't fire together, don't wire together. The cells lose their relationship, so every time you are able to interrupt a thought process, or an emotional state like anger, the nerve cells that are connected begin to break the long-term relationship. One of the easiest ways to break this pattern when you feel anger rising is to take a deep breath and say the word *release* out loud. From that space you can begin to reprogram and recondition your brain. You must become conscious and think about how you are acting and reacting to situations in your life. It's important to observe your habitual behavior and begin to address this one day at a time. Your anger is anchored to past events. In order to release and break your current state of being, you must commit to releasing your angry emotions from your present and your future.

Each of us has approximately 100 million brain cells. Everything that makes you *you*—your thoughts, dreams, hopes, fears, memories, pain, anger, joy—resides within the miracle that is your brain. Every day, as you learn and experience new things, your brain is at work making connections and essentially creating a "new you." As Dr. Joe Dispenza says:

The images that we create in our mind as we process different streams of consciousness leave footprints in the vast endless fields of neurological landscape, which contribute to the identity called "you." For the "you" as a sentient being is immersed and truly exists in the interconnected electrical web of cellular brain tissue. How our nerve cells are specifically arranged by what we learn, what we remember, what we experience, what we feel, what we envision, as well as what we think about ourselves defines us individually and it is reflected in our internal neurological wiring. We are a work in progress.[36]

Years ago scientists thought the brain was hardwired— you were born with a certain number of neurological connections and that was that. But technology has introduced functional imagery (functional magnetic resonance imagery), which measures brain activity in a way that wasn't possible before, and this has demonstrated that it is possible for the brain to work differently. Now scientists know that concentration and focus are skills that can be learned, just like tennis or playing the piano.

Functional imagery has proven that we can change our brains by thinking differently. We can activate new parts of our brains, creating new brain circuits. Other research has proven similar results in the body. Tests have shown that the mind-body connection is real; the mind is able to change the body. Physical changes result when we change our thoughts and intentions.

All of this is good news for releasing unresolved anger and overcoming addictions. To change a habit or an addiction, however, requires a level of honesty and objectivity that your ego initially may rebel against. Many people say they want to change and let go, but when faced with the facts, they prefer to stay disappointed. Most people aren't prepared to face the fact that they have been abandoned, abused, and neglected at different points in their lives, and these events leave feelings that eventually become an identity. Changing requires courage, new routines, and habits that will liberate you one day at a time.

You can't create a new present or a new future by holding onto the emotions of the past. Events from your past have created feelings and moods that have become your identity. And unless you know how to release unresolved negative emotions, you'll remain stuck in your anger and your addiction.

You must first remove yourself from the old events and begin to observe what's happening in your present. Make a powerful decision to respond differently. You can choose today who you want to be, how you want to live, and how you want to respond. Choosing positive change creates an energy that is greater than whatever negative addiction has you in its grip.

Ultimately the external world will no longer have the power to affect your personal reality. You can forge new connections. You can create new experiences, which shape new behaviors. You will experience new subconscious reactions, and you'll now be able to create a new reality, one that is free of addiction, free of anger. As you release your old, inhibiting beliefs and identity, new possibilities present themselves. You don't have to be chained to your past—you don't have to be an addict!

Quantum Healing

Quantum healing is a type of energy healing that utilizes natural methods to work with the powerful energy that exists within the body. This approach to healing was developed by Dr. Deepak Chopra in the 1980s. He was able to merge Western medicine, neuroscience, and physics in new ways that revealed how a network of intelligence in the body can alter patterns in our physiology.[37] His research impacted the way cancer and heart disease were treated, and further studies showed that this approach could also be successful in treating addictions.

This research shows that blockages form in our quantum energy body (i.e., spirit), accumulating after years of trauma, negative belief systems, anger, and addictions. Once those blockages are released, a new, positive energy is able to flow through us. We are able to release our addictions and experience alignment in our mind, body, and spirit. This alignment is essential to develop health and well-being in recovery. When we tap into our energy body, which exists in the quantum field of infinite possibilities, healing begins.

I have so much admiration for the work of Dr. Joe Dispenza because he is one of the few scientists to fully grasp the role of emotion in healing and releasing addiction. In fact, negative emotion is oftentimes an addiction to high levels of our own stress hormones. These hormones have set points, which explains why we feel out of our comfort zone when we think thoughts or explore beliefs that upset our hormonal balance. This idea is at the very core of the new scientific understanding of addictions and cravings. By changing your internal state, you can change your external reality.

The idea that you can release your addictions by translating thought into emotion might sound astounding at first. But there have been many documented instances where individuals have done just that. When combined with traditional ways of treating addictions, many individuals experience high levels of freedom and release.

The Law of Attraction

Whether you have low self-esteem or moderate self-esteem, recognize that you're in the process of changing. You can become more spiritual, more emotionally healthy. Give yourself the privilege of understanding the laws of vibration, the laws of the universe, the laws of attraction. Once you understand the basics, you'll be poised to cross over into *synchronicity*. According to Merriam-Webster's, *synchronicity* is actually a medical term meaning "the coincidental occurrence of events and especially psychic events (as similar thoughts in widely separated persons or a mental image of an unexpected event before it happens) that seem related but are not explained by conventional mechanisms of causality—used especially in the psychology of C. G. Jung."

With synchronicity there is no separation between you and the outcome. It implies oneness. You are not separate; you are unified. There's no disconnection between your emotional body and your mind.

Quantum physics has taught us a lot about the universe. The unseen world is more real—more powerful—than the world we see around us. In 2006 the movie *The Secret* was released. The whole film revolved around the law of attraction, which is basically the way the unseen world manifests itself in the situations and events of our lives.

In order to understand the law of attraction, we have to have an understanding of cause and effect. John Assaraf and Murray Smith, in their brilliant book *The Answer*, describe it like this:

> *An important client says yes or no. A substantial investment comes through or falls through. Real estate prices rise sharply or fall unexpectedly. Markets shift, hurricanes blow through, and new developments surprise us. We see and react to all these events without realizing they are but the seen tip of the unseen iceberg, the physical end results of a nonphysical process of creation. We often respond to these events without realizing the role that we ourselves play in bringing them about. We see the world of tangible phenomena; we don't see the vastly greater world that gives rise to it. That vastly greater world is the world of cause.*[38]

Clients tell me, "I don't know why I can't attract good relationships. I don't understand why I can never get ahead." I assist them to see how this type of self-talk is a direct reflection of their law of attraction. You attract who you are or someone who is in a lower vibrational state than you. I tell my clients they must raise their attractor factor.

The law of attraction has a core principle that says *you are the cause in your life*. Period. This is challenging for many of us because we are not used to feeling in control of our lives. It's much easier to relinquish responsibility and view someone else or some other outside situation as the cause of our misery and anger. But when you understand that you alone are the cause behind the effect, you no longer have the luxury of blaming someone else for what happens to you.

Healthy Habits for Recovering Addicts

Overcoming alcoholism, illegal or prescription drug abuse, food issues, and emotional addictions is challenging. Going through detox is never pleasant or easy. Releasing unresolved anger from past events is often a painful process. But on the other side of addiction, a new life awaits. In order to maintain an addiction-free lifestyle, new habit patterns are required. Here are five simple strategies you can incorporate now.

Develop an active lifestyle. This not only maintains your physical health and assists you in rebuilding a new identity, physical activity also has a huge effect on your emotional health. Even developing the habit of a daily walk in your neighborhood can make a substantial impact. But with your mind and heart free from the negative effects of addiction, you might also want to explore new forms of activity: take a yoga class, engage in water aerobics, or begin a weight-training program.

Develop good sleep habits. Sleep deeply and well. Depriving yourself of sleep has a very negative effect on the recovery process. Depleted energy levels are the result, and these can lead to those old negative emotions reasserting themselves. Poor sleep patterns have been linked to relapse among recovering alcoholics. While the amount of sleep we need differs, start by aiming for seven or eight hours a night. You'll be amazed at the difference waking up refreshed will make.

Retrain your eating habits. Start by deciding you will only eat when you are hungry. Eat slowly, really savoring the taste, texture, and aromas. Engaging all your senses will assist you to eat mindfully and stop when you're full. This will also improve your digestion.

Instead of trying to overcome emotions such as anger or sadness by eating something salty or sweet, you can focus on other food choices that are beneficial to your health and well-being.

Develop new hobbies and interests. As an addict, you most likely had some entrenched routines. Now that you have released your addiction, there is a void where those old routines used to be. To let go of an addiction, you must be willing to let go of the people that you associate with who perpetuate your addiction and the places you frequent that foster your addictive behavior.

No longer choosing to associate with those from your past drug or alcohol days requires new routines, new relationships, and new activities. Now is the time to explore new hobbies or interests that open up new avenues of constructive pursuits.

Explore your spirituality. Addicts are used to addressing their pain and anger with addictive substances or activities. Now in recovery, they must learn new ways to deal with any unresolved issues from past events. Exploring the spiritual side of life is one way to do this. Meditation, deep breathing, and prayer can benefit you in surprising ways. Enjoy the beauty of nature and get in touch with your own spirit.

Life Is More Than Producing

In my own recovery journey, I used to have challenges taking time off, taking vacations, and relaxing. I was consumed by reading personal development, self-help, and addiction books. I was committed to improving myself, being my best, going to meetings, events, workshops, rallies, and conventions. I felt guilty if I was not improving myself or producing.

After all the years I lost being an addict, I had very few hobbies or outlets to express myself other than "producing." That was the story I told myself. About ten years ago, however, I gave myself permission to change; I realized I deserved a life. I started to develop new habits; I reconnected with friends from my past who I had lost track of. I started developing my hobbies and taking time off for myself. I began reading fiction and doing more of what I love in life other than producing and succeeding. I realized how counterproductive it was to feel guilty whenever I relaxed. Today my identity is no longer what I do for my vocation. This has led to incredible freedom in my life.

Be Pro-Recovery

When you enter recovery and become rigorously honest

and committed to "No More Cheat Days," you have entered a level of emotional clarity where relapsing is not an option. As you let go of control, you are no longer controlling the control that keeps you addicted. Letting go of guilt, shame, and resentment allows you to not feel attached or controlled by yourself and others. Your success in life is dependent on your recovery.

To heal the addicted brain, change your thoughts and feelings from pro-addiction to pro-recovery. Let go of your inner critic that continues to validate the people who violated, abandoned, rejected, and created the brokenness that keeps you overwhelmed and addicted. You have suffered enough! There is so much life for you to live—stop wasting it on your past and live for today.

Breaking through is breaking down the cause that creates the effect. Breaking through requires letting go of events, people, and situations that have become an identity and an emotional addiction. Awareness of why you do what you do and then teaching yourself to interrupt a feeling in mid-moment will lead to a new set of feelings. Affirming that you are in recovery of any addiction is the foundation of letting go.

Transformation requires patience. If you are in the process of letting go of an addiction, patience becomes a skill to master. There are very few overnight success stories. Be willing to pay the price without knowing the cost. If you don't, you will constantly be starting over, paying the price of regret.

Do you know how good you are? Are you aware of how much greatness resides within you? Do you realize there are people waiting for you to show up, so they can show up? Cry tears of release rather than tears of pain, and give yourself permission to channel your inner brilliance. There is no longer any reason to struggle. Let go, release, and receive!

This is a journey that will expand your horizons of what is possible and challenge you to embrace a radically higher level of healing and functioning. Immerse yourself in the process and release the thoughts, feelings, and events that have limited you in the past. Believe in your ability to realize your highest potential and take action, and create the happy and healthy future you absolutely deserve.

Ask Yourself

1. *Am I willing to pay the price and release my addictions? Have I suffered enough?*

2. *If I find myself stuck in disappointment and regret, what steps can I take now to assist my recovery?*

3. *What new hobbies or interests might I enjoy exploring? Are there old friends that I've lost touch with that I'd like to contact?*

CHAPTER ELEVEN
FORGIVENESS: THE LANGUAGE OF THE HEART

Letting go begins with releasing the control that keeps you in the control of being out of control. That may sound paradoxical, but let me break that down for you. Control and letting go are relatively synonymous. Control is not something that is physical. It's more etherical; it belongs to the unseen energy that permeates all matter. It's letting go of the feelings you have and the feelings you create that form your identity.

If you are angry, if you are resentful, if you feel abandoned, rejected, and overwhelmed, or if you feel guilt or shame, letting go is not physical. If someone has physically or emotionally violated you, if a boss has mistreated you, or if a relative, spouse, or friend has wronged you, letting go begins with forgiveness.

Forgiveness is a decision. Forgiveness is a process. When you can say, "I let go," in a very relaxed state, then there is a high probability that you have neutralized the effects and the cause is no longer affecting you. Once you begin to do that, you forgive. You let go. You can create less significance with those events, people, and situations. Neurologically it's not part of your chemistry anymore.

As you learn to let go, you won't take situations personally. You stop giving power to people and situations that no longer have significance. But when you give significant significance to people and events that no longer serve you, that becomes part of your identity. You will continue to create the same situations over and over to attract to your reality people and situations that fulfill a set of feelings you have become neurologically and biochemically addicted to.

The key to letting go is forgiveness. Forgiveness is required in order to understand that a lot of your anger is stored from the past. You might say, "I don't remember my childhood. I don't remember how this happened." If that's true of you, chances are you will become just like the passive-aggressive anger addict that showed up in your own household. Anger creates sabotage because anger alienates people. When you are hostile, when you get upset, when you fly off the handle, when you don't have a stop button, when you're completely out of control, you're on your way to becoming a victim. And what if someone points out that you are a victim? You get angry.

Everything I'm sharing with you in this book I've been through myself. I experienced a series of transgressions as a child. When I was not able to perform to a certain set of standards, I understood very quickly that no matter what I did, it wasn't good enough. This same scenario happens to a lot of us because other people in our circle of influence have "an intention of good intentions." There's no rule book on how to be a perfect parent, just as there's no rule book on how to be a perfect coach or a perfect boss. In the end it's our responsibility to let go of the events that shaped those feelings that keep us doing the same thing over and over.

Forgiveness provides a huge release. When you forgive someone for what he or she did, it takes you off the hook. It also allows you to feel better about yourself. You don't have to physically confront someone to let go of your anger, however. You can write a letter. You can just simply let go of the individual. If you're sitting around waiting for a hug and a high five, or if you are waiting for that person to apologize to you, you're holding him or her responsible—you're the victim rather than the victor.

When you forgive and let go, you become victorious over the feelings you've held onto. This is the opposite of being the victim, playing the same blame, rage, resent, and overwhelm game over and over. You'll never get anywhere doing that. When you're attempting to attract prosperity or a life partner, you'll continue to attract the same kind of situations and people that are familiar.

Understanding Forgiveness

One reason many of us resist forgiveness is that we really don't understand it. We think we do—but we have a limited perception of how it actually works. It seems unfair, as though we're letting someone who hurt us off the hook with no consequences for his or her actions. We might think forgiving someone who abused or violated us means that we must invite that person into our life again; we might have to be friends with him or her. But these are just some of the misconceptions surrounding forgiveness. While forgiving those who wronged us is important, we should never feel we have to trust someone who violated our trust or choose to be around those who wounded us, without healthy boundaries.

Especially for those who have been abused and violated or emotionally abandoned, forgiveness can be difficult to cultivate. It seems so much more natural to hold yourself and others responsible for failures, mistakes, and hurts. But if you are able to forgive, it's one of the most rewarding experiences you'll ever have. When anger is released and forgiveness takes root in your heart, love will find you in a myriad of ways.

The experts who study forgiveness are clear about what forgiveness is—and what it is not. They are very specific in how they define forgiveness. Psychologist Sonja Lyubomirsky, a professor at the University of California, calls forgiveness "a shift in thinking" toward someone who has wronged you "such that your desire to harm that person has decreased and your desire to do him good (or to benefit your relationship) has increased."[39] At the very least forgiveness means that you make a conscious decision to let go of any desire for revenge or retaliation toward a person who has wronged you.

What Forgiveness Is Not

Before we can understand what forgiveness is, it's important to be clear on what it is not.

Forgiveness is not the same as reconciliation. While forgiveness might lead to eventually reconciling with the other party, it's also possible to forgive someone without choosing to continue the relationship. Forgiveness is up to you; it is not dependent on the other person, while reconciliation, on the other hand, is mutual.

Forgiving is not forgetting. The old saying goes, "Forgive and forget." But if you become focused on forgetting, you might find yourself back in denial, suppressing your true feelings. It is possible to forgive and still remember the hurt inflicted on you—but without anger or the need for revenge. Forgiving is not letting someone off the hook. Forgiveness is about giving yourself permission to release the pain so you can get on with your life. Forgiveness is taking responsibility for your present while releasing the significance you've attached to the past.

Forgiveness is not excusing a wrongdoer. When you forgive someone, this does not mean that you make light of, justify, or make excuses for the wrong that was done. It certainly doesn't mean denying the hurt or your feelings about what happened. And forgiveness absolutely does not mean putting yourself in harm's way again. You can forgive someone and still take healthy steps to protect yourself, including choosing not to reconcile. An example of this is a woman who courageously leaves an abusive spouse once and for all. She can choose to forgive, but she also doesn't minimize the danger or hurt she experienced.

Forgiveness does not mean becoming a victim again. It's not giving an offender permission to walk all over you. It's also not playing the part of a martyr. You are not meant to tolerate a lack of respect or any other form of abuse.

Forgiveness is not making sure justice is done. When an individual is sincerely sorry and apologizes for hurting someone else, it's obviously much easier to forgive that person. But often this is not the case. And it doesn't matter—it is separate from the act of forgiveness. You might forgive someone and still seek restitution. But whether or not you get the justice you seek, forgiveness is still your choice.

Forgiveness is not a one-time event. Forgiveness is actually a process. It may take time to come to the place where you are able to forgive an adult from your past for hurts visited upon you as a child. If you've endured a painful divorce, it might take time to be able to forgive the offending spouse. You can give yourself the time you require to process and heal. This is preferable to forgiving too quickly or superficially.

The Transformative Power of Forgiveness

I've become a student of forgiveness over the years, and I've studied it diligently. I've seen how transformative it has been in my own life. Forgiveness allows me to be objective in the moment, honest enough to ask questions such as:

How am I responsible for this event?

How can I heal?

How did I attract this situation?

What doors might open if I choose to forgive?

What will this teach me so I can teach others?

Forgiveness releases you—and it also releases others from your pain. It allows you to heal and love from your heart.

All the negative effects of anger are transformed into the positive benefits of forgiveness. People who are able to forgive typically have better health, more satisfying relationships, and higher self-esteem. Here are five initial steps to forgive those who have wronged you:[40]

Acknowledge the pain you feel. It hurts when someone violates your trust or wrongs you in some way. Unresolved anger masks that hurt, but when you let go of anger, you can then feel what you feel. It's the opposite of denial, which only blocks your path to freedom and forgiveness.

Work through any confusion. Anger colors your world; letting go of it involves being willing to look at your false perceptions and release false beliefs about what happened in the past.

Seek to understand. As difficult as this might be initially, once you let go of your anger, you can make the decision to begin to understand the facts about the event, which may have been colored by your angry perceptions. You can attempt to understand what might have happened in the life of the individual that wronged you. This doesn't lessen the offense or condone it, but it does open the door for your own healing process.

Allow yourself to grow in wisdom and insight. When you aren't hindered by self-pity, resentment, bitterness, and anger, you have the opportunity to move beyond your own pain and exercise forgiveness, which is courageous and powerful.

Choose to surrender the past event. As you are able to let go and forgive, you can move forward in a way that was previously not an option for you. You will experience release and a new sense of personal freedom.

Forgiving Yourself

It's one thing to forgive someone else, but it can be even more difficult to forgive yourself. Maybe you were the one who cheated on your spouse, became an alcoholic, neglected your kids, got in trouble with the law...then what?

One of the biggest obstacles to forgiving yourself is the tendency to be so caught up in guilt and shame that you wallow in it. Psychologist Fred Luskin, director of the Stanford University Forgiveness Project, says: "It's not just that we feel bad because we know we've done wrong; everybody does that. But some of us actually draw those bad feelings around ourselves like a blanket, cover our heads, and refuse to stop the wailing."[41]

Feeling bad becomes the way some people attempt to remove themselves from the consequences of their actions. Instead of taking responsibility for their mistakes, repairing the damage, and making things right, these individuals oftentimes unconsciously decide to punish themselves by feeling miserable for the rest of their lives.

Because our lives are so entwined, however, this can have serious consequences for our relationships. Someone who is miserable, wallowing in guilt, tends to be withdrawn, irritable, critical—and anyone in that person's path is bound to feel the brunt of those negative, angry emotions.

This way of dealing with your mistakes is a form of self-hatred, and it affects your physical and mental health in the same ways unresolved anger does. That's why not being able to forgive leads individuals to have a much higher risk of heart attacks, high blood pressure, and other serious health issues.

Forgiveness allows you to face what you've done in the past, acknowledge your mistakes, and move on. This does not mean that you make excuses or justify what happened. You might not ever forget what you did. But there comes a time when you must move past regret and start over. Here are some practical tips that can assist you to do that.[1]

Face your offenses. Some of the most difficult things to forgive are failing at something big, such as your marriage; hurting someone else due to your actions; indulging in self-destructive behavior like drinking or gambling; neglecting something important, such as saving for retirement or managing your finances. Facing into the severity of what you did—naming it—sets you on the path toward forgiveness. It gives you a bit of objectivity and distances you from the offense.

Confession is good for the soul. Being able to articulate what you did and how it affected others is vital. You might choose to share this with a trusted friend or coach, being open to any support or advice he or she might offer. Being transparent about your failings assists you to realize that we all make mistakes. Too often we feel alone in our anger and guilt, and that sense of isolation prevents healing. Being honest about events breaks the denial syndrome.

Release unrealistic expectations. When we have unresolved anger from past events, it leads to unconscious "rules" and beliefs about how we "should" behave. Those expectations often are unrealistic and do not serve us once we become adults.

For instance, take a child who was raised by a controlling mother who was difficult (if not impossible) to please. That child developed unconscious beliefs about the necessity of always giving in to her mother's demands, no matter how unreasonable. Then as an adult, when that now elderly mother requires extra assistance, the daughter might feel compelled to care for her mother in her own home, even though their every interaction is negative and upsetting. If that daughter can release her unrealistic expectations about how a daughter should respond to her mother, she might decide that a better course of action is to assist her mother to relocate to a facility with trained professionals who can care for her.

Identify the true source of the pain. All the anger, guilt, hurt, and stress you're experiencing now is causing you to feel miserable—not the event that happened yesterday or twenty years ago. Your reactions today are keeping you stuck, and releasing them frees you from the past. Replaying your mistake over and over is not productive either for you or the person or persons you hurt. Learn to refocus on the positive.

Be sincere and make amends. It takes courage to ask others to forgive you, but an honest apology can sometimes go a long way to repairing damaged relationships. Then look for ways to make amends. You can't change the past, but you absolutely can choose differently in the present. Instead of feeling bad, see if you can identify something good you can do. This can open the door to a whole new level of living.

Put things in perspective. Yes, maybe you've made a mess of things. But you also have acted in many good and honorable ways. Take some time each day to reflect on how you've made life easier for those around you. Beating yourself up about things you've done in the past can create a pretty painful present. Instead of being consumed with anger toward yourself, forgive yourself and begin to experience gratitude for who you are and all the good things in your life. As Dr. Luskin says, "It's so much better to do good than to feel bad."[42]

The Benefits of Forgiveness

As you let go of anger, bitterness, and resentment, in its place there is now room for a host of positive situations. The benefits of forgiveness are often surprising. For instance, studies have shown that releasing anger and bitterness toward someone who has wronged you has a positive effect on your physical stamina. Letting go leads to happiness, health, and peace. The benefits of forgiveness include:[43]

- Healthier relationships
- Greater spiritual and psychological well-being
- Less anxiety, stress, and hostility
- Lower blood pressure
- Fewer symptoms of depression

- Stronger immune system
- Improved heart health
- Higher self-esteem

No longer will you angrily define your life by how you've been hurt. When you exercise the power of forgiveness, you'll experience new levels of purpose and passion, and life will become the exhilarating adventure it is meant to be. It may even lengthen your life.

And as you let go of anger and forgive others for what has happened in the past, you'll create new patterns and habits of compassion and forgiveness that will serve you in the present. Forgiveness is required—often on a daily basis—for a peace-filled, joy-filled, love-filled existence.

The Silent Power of Love

Love is the most powerful force in the universe. When you love, you transmute and transmit an energy that transforms situations and people without you having to say a word. As we let go of our own anger and become willing to forgive, we can be agents of change and forgiveness in others. As David Hawkins says:

People who are hateful will, in our presence, suddenly become willing to forgive others. We can see the person transform right in front of us. Letting go of anger, they might say, "Well, there's no reason to be so mad at him...he's too young to know better." They will find an excuse to defend the person, instead of attacking him. Love empowers us, and the people around us, to do things that we would not be capable of otherwise.[44]

Forgiveness stems from love. We begin to see all of life differently. We see grace instead of judgment. We love ourselves; we forgive ourselves for past events and situations.

Forgiveness leads to gratitude—for life itself and all it contains. Forgiveness is one of the most powerful strengths you can possess. It's truly a gift you can give yourself that keeps on giving in unexpected ways. It's also a gift you can share with those in your sphere of influence. Forgiveness empowers you to let go freely and fully.

Ask Yourself

1. *Is there anyone in my life that requires my forgiveness?*

2. *Is there anyone I have wronged, anyone I must ask to forgive me?*

3. *How has forgiveness made a difference in my life?*

CHAPTER TWELVE

FROM ANGRY REACTOR
TO PEACEFUL RESPONDER

The goal of this book is to assist you to release anger and live in a state of peace. When you operate from peace, there is no more conflict. Without conflict, there is no longer any reason to cling to your anger. There is a lack of negativity, and in its place is peace, serenity, tranquility, and being present to the present. You are content. What are some other qualities you can expect to experience when anger is gone?

- Oneness
- Unity
- Freedom
- Lightness
- Fulfillment
- Joy
- Harmony

Just as anger comes along with a host of negative emotions and effects, the opposite of anger—peace and love—brings positive effects. A person who experiences inner peace can no longer be controlled, manipulated, coerced, intimidated, bullied, or marginalized. This is an enlightened state—the kingdom of mystics, saints, and sages. Before we go any further, let's take one last look at the anger-ridden state we are leaving behind.

The Not-Good-Enough Syndrome

Contrasted with this high plane of peacefulness, guilt, shame, worry, overwhelm, and control all lead to feelings of what I call NGE—the not-good-enough syndrome. When you live a large percentage of your life feeling not good enough, you'll attract people and situations to fulfill your need to stay disappointed. The answer is learning to master your emotional state, and it's not all that difficult to accomplish. You do not necessarily require therapy.

When you feel guilt and shame, you attract people who correspond to that low vibrational state or those who are beneath it. Attracting the lowest of the low then fulfills your feelings of guilt and shame. You'll only experience more guilt while you're busy attracting other guilt seekers in order for you to stay guilty. Guilt is the lowest transmutation of emotional etheric energy. When you find yourself in guilt, you're right back in the murkiness of being overwhelmed in your addictive emotional state, sadly wondering why you can't seem to get anywhere.

Mastering Your Emotional State

If you allow guilt seekers—those who live in guilt or in the very low vibrational energy of shame—to continue to affect your emotional state, you'll either resent them or go back to them out of guilt (and then you'll resent them anyway). Instead learn to let go of your control of the feelings that keep you in control; you have to let go of being in an addicted emotional state that keeps you overwhelmed. Being overwhelmed creates an energetic vibration that takes you to the top of the elevator. You have a little juice from dopamine, but then the bottom falls out and you're back in the shaft of the elevator in cortisol overwhelm wondering how you got there.

The idea of being positive puts a lot of pressure on people to be and stay positive all the time. That's not possible, and here's why. When you must be positive at all times, it conditions you to repress any anger that might appear, and if you repress your anger, it turns into unresolved anger. You might even feel guilty about being negative and angry—and then feel guilty about being guilty. If this is your emotional state, it's going to be very challenging for you to attract people who are relaxed, collaborative, and spiritual, people who can connect. Instead you'll only encounter those who have emotional challenges.

It's not about perfection, but it does require the ability to become very skilled at your emotional state. Being able to master your emotional state is a skill you unequivocally want to develop. That way, when you feel yourself slipping into a familiar negative state, you won't let yourself get overwhelmed by it. When your meltdown is really a "melt-up," you catch yourself melting down, but then you'll bring yourself right back up. You'll have a *mini* breakdown, not *many* breakdowns.

The real question is: How do you stop the insanity? How do you become free of angry tendencies? It requires taking a good look at why you do what you do. If you're in this kind of state, there's a high probability you are trapped in inaction and procrastination. This book about anger builds upon the last book I wrote, *From Procrastination to Production*, because typically when you're in an overwhelmed emotional state and living with habitual anger, you don't use your time wisely and have a tendency to procrastinate. Underlying the inability to move forward and do what is required is unresolved anger and low self-esteem.

Comfortable in Your Own Skin

What is the opposite of low self-esteem? It's not *high* self-esteem—it's *healthy* self-esteem. Self-esteem means that you are comfortable with who you are. You're comfortable with what you're becoming; you're comfortable with where you are going. You're comfortable in your own skin. You are happy being you, and you are free.

With healthy self-esteem, there's no separation between you and results. There is no separation between you and the emotional states of joy, love, peace, bliss, and enlightenment. When separation exists, you are in a very low vibrational emotional state that sends out a mixed message saying, "Please violate me. Please show up and disappoint me. Please seduce me into believing that you and I are going to have a long-term relationship even though I know eventually you're going to leave me."

This all has to do with the way you were conditioned

175

to behave. You did what you had to do, but because that became your identity and became a component of your neurological network, you haven't been able to separate yourself from the events that led to this situation. The events that you hold onto and the way you perceive them will create your identity. When you live in an angry, guilt-ridden space, you'll attract other codependent individuals who will fulfill your disappointment.

Being brutally honest, I've been there. I'm an addict, and I also have a codependent personality. I'm proud to state that I'm in recovery from both of these situations. They are two different addictions. Even though I achieved sobriety from one addiction, I relapsed in the other. This led to me gaining a better understanding of why I am codependent—why I set people up to disappoint me.

If you have a similar tendency, it means that when you attract someone into your circle of influence, you start to paint a picture of him or her that's bigger than where you are. You are not meeting the person where he or she is. You're virtually setting that person up to disappoint you.

If you're worried about how this person is going to pull it off, you might start doing things for him or her. For instance, you might begin giving the person money. As you do more and more things for this individual, you're essentially setting the stage for him or her to disappoint you. That's often where the romance goes sideways because the person begins to feel your control. You both end up being out of control, and so one of you leaves the relationship because you can already tell it's going to be dysfunctional. This is an example of how you set yourself up to be disappointed.

You're superman. You're superwoman. You can say yes, yes, yes, but you don't know diplomatically how to say no. Just recently I experienced some of this myself. My Breakthrough to Success event this past December was the largest Breakthrough I've ever hosted. I turned down over twenty-one people that wanted to attend this event, and even though I know it loses its intimacy if there are too many people, I experienced feelings of guilt. "Oh no, I'm denying someone a breakthrough." However, in actuality there's also one in February. There's one in June. There's one in September. There are regular opportunities for individuals to experience breakthroughs at one of these events.

Sometimes I get emotionally intoxicated in my own codependent state. I want to empower people, rescue people, and put them in a position to breakthrough. I've had to learn the meaning of the word *boundary*. I have had to create boundaries involving dedicated blocks of time to different areas of production. I also devote time to areas of charity, blocks of time where I do service work with addicts, alcoholics, and people in recovery. I've learned the hard way that I can't be available 24/7.

I used to be "Delta, delta, delta—let me help you, help you, help you. Call me anytime; I'll give you the shirt off my back. My store is open 24/7; just call me. I'm Ronnie the Rescuer." I used to be the King Kong of rescuing: 1-800-RescueU—that's how I fulfilled my low self-esteem. Before I overcame this, I would think to myself, *Wow, I'm really doing great service out there in the world while I'm broke. I'm giving my time away.*

It's not a black-and-white world. Service is important. It's important that you give value to others. It's important that you care about the common man, are concerned about those less fortunate than you. It's important to pull over to the side of the road and assist someone with a flat tire. It's important to give blood. It's important that you do your civic duty. It's good to open doors for women and children and elders and salute the flag and be a good, old-fashioned, red-blooded American. All these things are valuable, but you must guard against an identity that's addicted to giving; you must also be able to receive.

Finding the Balance

You have to find balance in the equation. That's why it's so important to let go of both your anger and your guilt. Guilt plays a large role in the American economy. Only a small percentage of the population ever breaks through and becomes truly financially successful. Success is like beauty—it's in the eye of the beholder. But when it comes to the laws that govern money, only a small percentage of the population has the majority of the wealth. In terms of net worth in America, only one-twentieth of one percent of the population has a net worth of $1 million or more.

And that doesn't mean that those people make a million dollars in a calendar year. That's an even smaller percentage of the population. The average American millionaire is part of a very, very small percentage of

Americans. This is a basic principle called "the law of the few."

I'm guessing that if you're reading this book, you are one of the success seekers—someone who really aspires to do something with your life. Maybe you want to empower others—you want to be able to teach, coach, speak, write, brand, or blog. If you're one of these people, you're spiritually inclined and you really want to do good for mankind; you want to assist and empower other people. If this describes you, you are in the minority.

A large percentage of the population is going to criticize you for the internal fortitude and courage to do what others won't so you can assist other people that can't. You'll have to toughen up because there will be those who attempt to use guilt to control you. If you have been conditioned to be guilted, there's a high probability that you will feel guilty about breaking through—and you will tend to sabotage yourself just when you're about to reach for the prize. This is just one more effect of unresolved anger issues.

You might also discover something about success, just like I did. I learned that success wasn't nearly as exciting as I thought it would be. I envisioned this magical, mythical finish line that I'd reach. Early in my speaking career, I thought all the biggest companies would come knocking on my door. I experienced a quick dose of reality: My first year I only spoke six times. I then realized that for me to be a professional speaker, I had to build my own database. I built my original speaking career while I ran my coaching business, and from day one I had at least a six to eight week waiting list, and sometimes as much as twelve to sixteen weeks.

I've always been an exceptional coach one-on-one, but speaking in front of a group was a whole different equation. I realized that for me to deliver my message required a growing circle of influence. My attractor factor began to change the more I understood quantum physics, quantum leaps, neuroscience, cause and effect, why we do what we do, how we stay addicted in an emotional state—and most importantly, the two key concepts of *freedom* and *letting go*.

Letting go isn't physical. It's non-linear. It's not something you do; it's who you are. It's not a how to. People repeatedly ask me, "How do I, how do I, how do I...how do you?" But the question is not *how*; it's *why* don't I. The more you understand why you do what you do, the higher the probability you will be able to let go.

Playing in a New Emotional Space

Letting go of control and struggle gives you a whole different emotional space to play in. Instead of only one or two personality types your ego feels comfortable controlling, the whole world opens up to you. No longer will you operate in codependency, only interacting with the type of person who fulfills your disappointment.

Your story becomes your identity. When you begin to change your story, you let go of all those entrenched beliefs that have become your identity. Your beliefs create your sense of certainty. You say you don't know why you can't attract the type of people you require, but you're certain about attracting those who enable you to continue to attract the same situation over and over, fulfilling your disappointment and eventually leading to overwhelm. You never really get anywhere. This is why letting go is so important.

Most of society just wants a recipe. They want a blueprint. They want you to tell them what to do because they've always been told what to do; they've always lived out of their left brain. And when they've been told what to do, they can go on hiding in guilt and shame.

Most of society has been conditioned to read from left to right, which means we learn to access our left brain first. We get rewarded for being in our left brain. Our educational system revolves around this conditioning. Many issues stem from operating from the left side of your brain.

Many parents, for instance, end up in debt because they get seduced into taking out college loans for their children. It all seems to make sense; it sounds logical and realistic. This thinking goes, *Well, of course I'll go into debt for $160,000. I have to give my child a college education (that he won't use) so I can feel guilt and shame, be overwhelmed, and pay with funds that don't exist.* When these individuals have tiptoed quietly through life and have no money left, they will feel even guiltier because they have been conditioned into being guilty.

It's crucial to understand that guilt is one of the biggest control mechanisms around. You have to become aware of how you've been guilted throughout a large percentage of your life. You've been guilted to go to college, get a job, and go into debt. You've been coerced into becoming involved in situations you don't really want to be a part of, and then you feel angry and resentful for getting duped into saying, "Yes, yes, yes. I'll do that. I'll be there. I'll pick up the kids. I'll watch your dog. I'll serve on that committee. I'll host the dinner. I'll take on another project. I'll drive across town, across the city, across the street, across the country, whatever you need. Yes, yes, yes. I'm here to help you, help you, help you."

Step Off the Hamster Wheel

This becomes extremely exhausting and overwhelming. Often you do not get the recognition you deserve, and that just results in more resentment. Does this describe your situation? Are you one of the multitudes trapped in a job you don't like, trading time for dollars? Are you okay with not getting overtime, consistently putting in sixty to eighty hours a week for someone else? Do you commute two or three hours in heavy city traffic each way, leaving you very little time to really live and enjoy life? Yet are you still just barely getting by, feeling resentful about not getting compensated for what you're worth? Are you envisioning a vastly different type of life and livelihood? What's the answer?

Just quit.

Yes, I realize how radical this sounds. However, at some point you have to step off the hamster wheel. Yes, this takes courage. You have to learn to address your addiction. You have to be comfortable with being uncomfortable. You have to address the cause that creates the effect. This requires intestinal fortitude—a quality that never goes out of fashion.

Success has a tendency to show up other people who aren't success seekers. When you have the courage to step out of the pack, people around you feel threatened and try to control you. They'll use smart remarks. They'll use logic to see if they can provoke you. It takes fortitude and high self-esteem, but you must learn neurologically not to relapse back into an emotional state of justifying, validating, and explaining—you have to let go of trying to beg people to understand, becoming angry or frustrated with them, or spending precious energy attempting to convince them.

Begin to access your right brain, your creative mind, your emotional side where your extrasensory perception, your intuition, resides. Tap into your ability to go beyond thinking and connect with feeling, touching, sensing. Move into the know state. Be innovative! You cannot be innovative when you're in the very low vibrational state known as guilt and shame.

Anger, guilt, and shame rob you of your creativity. It keeps you in a place where you're in a constant state of worry. It keeps you living in the unknown state. You live in a place where you get ready to get ready. You're not sure if you can pull it off. You worry about worry, and you're worried about what happens if you were to let go of worry—because what would you worry about if you weren't worrying? I've actually had clients say to me, "Well, if I let go of my worry, how am I going to occupy my space?" Is that the zone you belong in?

If you live in an overwhelmed state, full of worry, anger, guilt, and shame, you're bound to feel uncomfortable with success. You don't feel you deserve it. You can't ask for an order, ask for a commitment, ask for seconds, ask for a parking space, ask for directions—you don't want to bother someone, or upset someone, or offend someone. These are the stories you tell yourself to stay overwhelmed and average. Guilt and shame lead to averageness. And deep down they result in a huge amount of unresolved anger.

If you tiptoe quietly through life—just an average Joe, an average Jane, an average Jack, an average Jean—there's a high probability you will resent other people who have the courage to not be average. I used to be Jeff with a chip on his shoulder. I had a little boulder sitting right there on my left shoulder. I carried that chip on my shoulder, and it got heavier and heavier each time someone relatively new would achieve success. They would get all kinds of positive acclaim while I wasn't getting any. I wasn't getting any recognition. I wasn't getting the reward—because I didn't earn it.

Attract a New Circle of Influence

As you let go of your anger and live in a new emotional state, I highly recommend that you develop a new circle of influence. Seek out individuals that will support and encourage you. Look for people who can offer unique perspectives and assist you to grow.

Develop your why. You have to have a *why* that is larger than your *what*. Spend less time on what and how—and more time on why. Simon Sinek wrote a great book entitled *Start with Why*. He says that asking why is "a naturally occurring pattern, a way of thinking, acting and communicating that gives some leaders the ability to inspire those around them."[45] He shows how asking why leads to being innovative. Innovation is creativity. It's the opposite of being logical and analytical.

Learn to rely on yourself. Get to the place where you can say with confidence:

> *"I am free. I am one with the universe."*
> *"I am intuitive. I sense. I feel. I taste."*
> *"I'm emotional. I am a spiritual being."*

When you come from that state, you're no longer disempowered. When you are separate, your emotional tank is very low. Your thoughts run along these lines:

> *"Oh, I'm having such a bad day."*
> *"I can't believe how my body looks."*
> *"I can't believe I relapsed last night."*

Especially when it comes to food issues, other people will guilt you into a relapse. I've had numerous clients say to me, "Oh, wow! I went to your seminar Saturday. It was amazing. Then I met my mom for dinner. We went to a restaurant and she started pushing my buttons, and…

well…that upset me. I found myself eating all the wrong things and drinking too much."

What happens next? The person goes over the cliff. Once over that cliff, there's no stopping when you're an addict. That is called a full-fledged binge. It very commonly shows up with food. You have to be able to eat smaller portions. You have to change your identity regarding your addiction. This is when the concept of separation becomes important. You learn to separate yourself from the feelings that led to your addiction. You have to be able to separate yourself and change your identity in terms of your addiction.

If you have lived a large percentage of your life in anger, anxiety, fear, and doubt, there's a high probability that you're going to feel behind in life. You're going to feel cheated. You're going to be angry at yourself. The most common anger is self-anger, which often turns into self-hatred, and self-hatred manifests itself in cutting, burning, drugs, alcohol, compulsive spending, gambling, and a multitude of negative situations.

Once you've mastered the art of letting go, however, you begin to be skilled at a new way of responding versus reacting. You become a peaceful responder instead of an angry reactor.

From Confrontation to Carefrontation

In life you will encounter many situations where there is conflict. You will be tempted by irritations, annoyances, and frustrating situations. You will often be troubled by other people's behavior. Instead of getting angry, confrontation will be required to create a resolution. You don't have to tolerate these situations because you are releasing anger. Not confronting can lead to repressed feelings and anger, which is the opposite of what you are attempting to achieve. Realize that confrontation can be very positive when you express yourself appropriately to others.

Confrontation is a skill, especially when you learn *carefrontation*. This is a term I invented myself, and it means that I care enough about myself and I care enough about others to be able to hold a mirror to their face and say, "Here! Look what you are doing." Carefrontation can also mean that I care enough about you to point this out.

Confrontation has more than one meaning. It does not mean that you "throw down on someone." It does not mean you are in control of controlling someone. Confrontation doesn't mean you are determined to be right. Confrontation means you are able to confront a situation.

Confrontation can be a necessary requirement in order to communicate your feelings about a situation. In confrontation, one of the keys is negotiating to find a resolution. In confrontation, oftentimes you can create a win-win situation. You can also back out of a confrontational situation in such a way that you don't feel like you lost. There is no win-win or lose-lose in confrontation.

A lot of your ideas and perceptions about confrontation bring up rejection and abandonment issues. In my own process of releasing anger and engaging in confrontation, I'd be remiss if I didn't tell you that I've lost my composure a time or ten. I lost my composure and slipped from confrontation into my old unresolved anger and created a situation that was not favorable. I wasn't always able to unwind it. That, my friends, is the human factor. When you have anger, resentment, guilt, shame, abandonment, rejection, overwhelmed feelings, and unresolved anger, that's a component of the situation.

Confrontation should come from a relaxed perspective. It should come from prosperity and reciprocity, but if you come from control and anger, if you have to be right, you only set yourself up for disappointment.

The skill of being able to confront comes from being able to be in the moment with people. The more you understand how to *carefront* from a confrontation perspective, the better you will be in control of your emotional state. When you are able to use diplomacy, you will have a much higher probability of creating a result, a resolution, and a solution in a relaxed, energetic state.

When you are engaging in a situation that requires confrontation, begin by defining the issue or challenge. Let the person know where change is required and articulate the benefits of resolving the issue. Be open to listening to the other person's thoughts and feelings without judgment.

Do your best to be clear in your language style. Beware of phrases such as "you always" or "you never." These statements are too generalized and will put the other person on the defensive. Be sure to address the effect the person's behavior is having on you without labeling the behavior with adjectives like "childish" or "annoying."

It's also important to consider your body language. Crossing your arms, rolling your eyes, and other facial expressions can interfere with creating a favorable outcome. The other person receives these nonverbal cues as negative feedback and is likely to become defensive instead of open to resolving the conflict.

When the other person speaks, it's important to listen. It will be very tempting to interrupt, but if you do this, the other person will not feel heard. Do your best to listen to what the other person is saying instead of trying to decide what you are going to stay next.

Occasionally you will encounter people that are sensitive and defensive. Do your best to recognize these people and realize they have a tendency to deflect or try to guilt you. This may create a situation where you must diplomatically disengage from the conversation if the opportunity for a resolution does not seem probable.

Another situation you may encounter is a person who becomes aggressive. This may be very similar to the "old you." Now that you are the "new you," you are able to stay calm, not take the bait, keep your voice at a normal speaking level, and be a peaceful responder. This is definitely a situation that may require diplomatically dismissing yourself. This may be an instance where you require letting go of the relationship or keeping your distance.

In today's society, email, texting, voicemail, Facebook, Twitter, Linkedin, and other social media outlets can provoke conflict or miscommunication. Often feelings of anger are triggered, and you may write a response or leave a message that you later regret. If confrontation is required, it's best to have a conversation by phone or in person rather than by typing a response. Much communication gets lost in translation through typing. You may misinterpret the person's tone or misunderstand what they mean. By having a live conversation, the line of communication is clear.

As you begin to step into your power, you can become a master at navigating confrontation. Your power zone is really about your emotional state. When you're in your power, you don't get rattled, you don't get overwhelmed, and you are not speaking anxiety into existence to fulfill your feelings. As you learn to confront and carefront diplomatically, you let go of your conflict consciousness with ease.

The Freedom Zone

What does life look like when you live from peace instead of anger? For one thing, the outside world no longer is your primary source of fulfillment; you know now that the true source of happiness is within. Because anger is no longer your identity, you are able to be supportive of others—you are kind, tolerant, loving, forgiving, and patient. Where once you were threatened by others and suspicious of their motives, now you see them as valuable and full of worth. Relationships and events seem to flow effortlessly. There is no need to be a struggleaholic any longer. Instead of one long string of challenges, life becomes a steady stream of opportunities. Let's look at some of the qualities you can expect to exhibit as you move into peace.

Peaceful responders experience gratitude and appreciation for life. When they set goals, they are confident they will achieve them. They know how to plan, and they are no longer victims of procrastination. Peaceful responders are fully alive and fully aware. Along with awareness comes an inner calmness and stillness.

Peaceful responders acknowledge the full spectrum of their emotions. They are not afraid to take emotional risks. They recognize that it's okay to not be perfect, and they are willing to be vulnerable. If they make a mistake, they are quick to admit it and then move on.

Peaceful responders allow others to be themselves. They don't insist that those around them act perfectly; they accept people, faults and all. They don't expect everyone to agree with them all the time; they don't ride herd on their significant other or their children. They recognize that theirs is not the only legitimate viewpoint.

Peaceful responders are assertive without being aggressive. They say what is required in a direct, forthright manner, without any hostility. They also don't feel the need to be in control at all times. They allow others to take the lead. They welcome contribution. They know how to listen; they participate in conversations without dominating them.

Peaceful responders are flexible. Like a successful boxer, a peaceful responder knows how to roll with the punches. Peaceful responders know how to choose their reactions depending upon the circumstances. They pick the response that seems most appropriate in any given situation.

Peaceful responders have the ability to think clearly. Instead of jumping to conclusions, they look at events from all sides. They think creatively; they don't see everything as all black or all white.

Peace Is Power

Being able to release toxic anger and operate in a state of peace opens up a whole new level of living. Instead of power struggles, agitation, irritation, and aggravation, you now have an easygoing, welcoming acceptance of others. No longer anxious and uptight, you are relaxed, full of energy, and radiant. Life unfolds in an effortless way. Feelings of gratitude, appreciation, pleasure, and confidence have replaced fear, anger, and struggle.

Moving out of your pain, you now start to move into your peace—and peace is where your power resides. You are finally able to become who you already are. You become a conduit for peace; this peace resonates from deep within you. It's an inside job; it's your very being. When you live from this place, you can create that environment anywhere. Whether you're stuck in a traffic jam, or something blows up at work, or you encounter a health issue, you can still operate from an environment of peace.

You will attract amazing people and situations to your reality when you live this way. Doors will open; people will seek you out; opportunities will present themselves. You—yes, you—will have an invisible energy that others are attracted to and want to be a part of.

Enjoy the journey—your dreams are waiting for you!

Ask Yourself

1. *Pick an area where you have been an angry reactor, and commit to letting go of your anger right now. First describe the situation, and then answer the question: What does being a peaceful responder in this situation look like?*

2. *Is there someone in your life that you have to confront? How can you use carefrontation in this situation?*

3. *As you move from anger to peace, make a list of the positive changes you see in your life.*

NOTES

1. http://www.wordcentral.com/cgi-bin/student?sabotage.
2. Ken Page, "An Interview with Marianne Williamson," *Psychology Today*, January 22, 2012. https://www.psychologytoday.com/blog/finding-love/201201/interview-marianne-williamson
3. Ronald T. Potter-Efron, *Angry All the Time, Second Edition: An Emergency Guide to Anger Control* (Oakland, Calif.: New Harbinger Publications, Inc, 2004) p. 24
4. Potter-Efron, p.26
5. David R. Hawkins, MD, PhD, *Letting Go: The Pathway to Surrender* (Carlsbad, Calif.: Hay House, 2012), p. 329.
6. Potter-Efron, p.43.
7. https://ncadd.org/about-addiction/drugs/prescription-drugs.
8. http://www.addictionrecov.org/Addictions/?AID=41.
9. http://www.addictionrecov.org/Addictions/?AID=34.
10. Acts 20:35
11. http://www.angriesout.com/family1.htm.
12. Signe Whitson, LSW, "Confronting Passive-Aggressive Behavior," *Psychology Today*, May 4, 2013. https://www.psychologytoday.com/blog/passive-aggressive-diaries/201305/confronting-passive-aggressive-behavior
13. http://www.huffingtonpost.co.uk/dan-roberts/how-to-be-assertive-not-p_b_1363244.html.
14. http://en.wikipedia.org/wiki/Terrell_Owens.
15. This information has been excerpted and paraphrased from Coaching Positive Performance (http://www.coachingpositiveperformance.com/8-examples-passive-aggressive-behaviour/)

16. Potter-Efron, p. 213.
17. Ibid.
18. See *Alcoholics Anonymous Comes of Age: A Brief History of AA*, 1957.
19. Louise Hay, *You Can Heal Your Body* (Carlsbad, Calif.: Hay House, 1984).
20. The following information has been adapted from David R. Hawkins' book *Letting Go*, pp. 216–217.
21. https://www.psychologytoday.com/blog/the-athletes-way/201301/cortisol-why-the-stress-hormone-is-public-enemy-no-1.
22. http://www.webmd.com/balance/stress-management/features/how-anger-hurts-your-heart.
23. http://www.webmd.com/heart-disease/features/rein-in-rage-anger-heart-disease.
24. University of Sydney. "Keep calm, anger can trigger a heart attack!" *ScienceDaily*, 24 February 2015. www.sciencedaily.com/releases/2015/02/150224083819.htm.
25. http://www.naturalnews.com/026727_liver_emotion_cleansing.html#.
26. http://howtoraiseyourvibration.blogspot.com/2011/05/liver-cleanse-releases-anger-from-past.html.
27. http://eatingdisordersreview.com/nl/nl_edr_14_5_8.html.
28. http://www.everydayhealth.com/diet-nutrition/food-and-mood/your-attitude/stop-eating-your-anger.aspx.
29. http://www.courtneypool.com/2013/11/how-anger-and-compulsive-eating-are-related.html.
30. https://www.nationaleatingdisorders.org/binge-eating-disorder.
31. Hawkins, p. 229.

32. http://www.drweil.com.
33. http://www.brainhq.com/brain-resources/everyday-brain-fitness/physical-exercise.
34. https://yogainternational.com/article/view/the-real-meaning-of-meditation.
35. http://sdintegrativemedicine.com.
36. http://drjoedispenza.com/index.php?page_id=the_brain_map_to_future.
37. See "The Dawn of the New Age of Addiction Recovery," http://www.connectthepieces.org/blog/135.
38. John Assaraf and Murray Smith, *The Answer: Grow Any Business, Achieve Financial Freedom, and Live an Extraordinary Life* (New York: Atria, a division of Simon & Schuster, Inc., 2008) p. 23.
39. http://www.pbs.org/thisemotionallife/topic/forgiveness/understanding-forgiveness.
40. Adapted from the book *When You Can't Say "I Forgive You,"* by Grace Ketterman and David Hazard (Colorado Springs: Nav Press, 2000).
41. http://www.prevention.com/print/mind-body/emotional-health/how-forgive-yourself-no-matter-what.
42. Ibid.
43. http://www.mayoclinic.org/healthy-lifestyle/adult-health/in-depth/forgiveness/art-20047692.
44. Hawkins, p. 175.
45. Simon Sinek, *Start with Why: How Great Leaders Inspire Everyone to Take Action* (New York: Penguin Books, 2009).

JEFFERY COMBS is an internationally recognized trainer, speaker, and best-selling author in the areas of sales, marketing, branding, and addiction. Jeff specializes in prospecting, leadership, scripts, spirituality, personal breakthroughs, mindset training, consciousness, and all levels of effective marketing. His many audio training programs benefit entrepreneurs and direct sales people at all levels of conscious development.

Jeff has consulted with over 9,000 clients as a personal coach and mentor and has devoted over 55,000 hours to his personal coaching practice. He is highly sought after by entrepreneurs, direct sales people, network marketers, and people from all walks of life. The president of Golden Mastermind Seminars Inc., Jeff is committed to assisting people change the way they feel in order to achieve their goals and dreams.

Jeff is available to you and your company for coaching and speaking, and he has developed a special package of training materials and professional guidance that will assist you and your team to create maximum results now. For further information, please call 800-595-6632 or visit his website at www.goldenmastermind.com.

YOU DESERVE TO HAVE IT ALL!

Personal Coaching
Producers Package
with **Jeffery Combs**

Jeffery Combs is the President and CEO of Golden Mastermind Seminars Inc. He is an internationally recognized trainer, speaker, and best-selling author specializing in sales, marketing, branding, and addiction. He has personally coached thousands of entrepreneurs and industry leaders, and he is committed to assisting people to change the way they feel in order to achieve their goals and dreams. Jeffery specializes in a 2-1/2 day workshop called Breakthroughs To Success. This is an absolute must for anyone desiring to go to the next level.

The Producers Package Includes:

- 5 Hours Personal Coaching with Jeffery Combs
- 1 Breakthroughs To Success Weekend Event Ticket
- 1 Digital Mastermind Library

800-595-6632
www.GoldenMastermind.com

GOLDEN MASTERMIND SEMINARS, INC.
THE DIGITAL MASTERMIND LIBRARY

With over 100 hours of content from Jeffery Combs and his guest
speakers, this is your ULTIMATE empowering training library! Owning
the complete Mastermind Library is a must for anyone serious about
building an enterprise!

- Receive Full Access to the **NEW** Digital Library at 65% OFF
- 22 training audios, 6 e-books, and The Millionaire Tip Lab
- All content is now MOBILE FRIENDLY!
- Receive New, Never Before Seen Training from Jeff's
  Archives!

Total Retail Value Exceeds $2,000.00!
Special *Anger Factor* Discounted Offer Only $697.00

www.GoldenMastermind.com/platinum-level-access